Digital Countercultures and the Struggle for Community

The Information Society Series

Laura DeNardis and Michael Zimmer, Series Editors

Interfaces on Trial 2.0, Jonathan Band and Masanobu Katoh

Opening Standards: The Global Politics of Interoperability, Laura DeNardis, editor

The Reputation Society: How Online Opinions Are Reshaping the Offline World, Hassan Masum and Mark Tovey, editors

The Digital Rights Movement: The Role of Technology in Subverting Digital Copyright, Hector Postigo

Technologies of Choice? ICTs, Development, and the Capabilities Approach, Dorothea Kleine

Pirate Politics: The New Information Policy Contests, Patrick Burkart

After Access: The Mobile Internet and Inclusion in the Developing World, Jonathan Donner

The World Made Meme: Public Conversations and Participatory Media, Ryan Milner

The End of Ownership: Personal Property in the Digital Economy, Aaron Perzanowski and Jason Schultz

Digital Countercultures and the Struggle for Community, Jessa Lingel

Digital Countercultures and the Struggle for Community

Jessa Lingel

The MIT Press
Cambridge, Massachusetts
London, England

This book was set in ITC Stone Sans Std and ITC Stone Serif Std by Toppan Best-set Premedia Limited. Printed and bound in the United States of America.

Library of Congress Cataloging-in-Publication Data

Names: Lingel, Jessa.
Title: Digital countercultures and the struggle for community / Jessa Lingel.
Description: Cambridge, MA : MIT Press, [2017] | Series: The information society series | Includes bibliographical references and index.
Identifiers: LCCN 2016037856 | ISBN 9780262036214 (hardcover : alk. paper)
Subjects: LCSH: Internet--Social aspects--United States. | Internet users--United States. | Subculture--United States. | Social interaction--United States. | Digital media--United States.
Classification: LCC HN90.I56 L56 2017 | DDC 302.23/10973--dc23 LC record available at https://lccn.loc.gov/2016037856

10 9 8 7 6 5 4 3 2 1

Contents

Acknowledgments

For giving me a love of reading and always encouraging my writing, I am permanently indebted to my parents, Craig and Robin Lingel. I also am indebted to my siblings and their partners—CJ, Kim, Anna, Amilia, and Dante. While struggling to write a book about the margins, I have consistently had my family as my center.

As a qualitative project, this research was possible only because of the openness and support of participants from the communities that I have studied. I am deeply grateful to all of my interviewees for their time and hope that I have done right by them in my analysis.

This book grew out of several collaborative projects. In 2009, I started a project on New Brunswick punk with Aaron Trammell, Nathan Graham, Joe Sanchez, and Mor Naaman. In 2011, I worked with danah boyd as an intern at Microsoft Research New England on *Body Modification Ezine* (BME), and her mentorship has profoundly influenced my work and career. Adam Golub first brought me to Brooklyn's drag community. I also am deeply grateful to Mark Hansen and Michael Kirsch from the Brown Institute for their support and friendship while researching this community. These brief mentions are woefully insufficient given the support that I have received from these individuals. Any errors in this book are mine alone.

Most of the book's manuscript was written while I was doing postdoctoral work at Microsoft Research New England in Cambridge, MA, and I am grateful to a number of lab colleagues for their friendship and feedback: Nancy Baym, danah boyd, Kate Crawford, Kevin Driscoll, Meg Finn, Tarleton Gillespie, Mary Gray, Rebecca Hoffman, Sham Kakade, Tero Karppi, Eva Lyubich, Annette Markham, Kate Miltner, Greg Minton, Jonathan Sterne, and Siva Vaidhyanathan. I am also deeply grateful to Jennifer

Chayes and Christian Borgs for their support of my work during my time at Microsoft Research.

After my postdoc fellowship, I moved to the Annenberg School at the University of Pennsylvania, where I am grateful to be part of a rich and rigorous academic community. I am particularly thankful for support from Sharrona Pearl, Kelly Fernandez, Marwan Kraidy, and Joe Turow.

A number of friends and colleagues provided comments and advice on this manuscript at various stages, including Sarah Banet-Weiser, Jack Bratich, Jack Gieseking, Germaine Haleguoa (my office spouse!), Dave Hesmondhalgh, Brian Hurley, Henry Jenkins, Michelle Lipinski, and Raz Schwartz. Michelle Mariano provided sage advice and much-needed editing. At the MIT Press, Gita Manaktala has been supportive of this project from the outset, and I am very grateful for her enthusiasm and support.

Writing this book was sometimes wonderful and sometimes agonizing. I am grateful to Warren Allen, Sylvia Bierhuis, Stephen Bolles, Suesan Cota, Kirk Vader, Laura Wade, and Ryan Wilson for supporting (and putting up with) me in various forms and moods in the last two years. Thanks also to Rinaldo Dorman and Sara Marx: Boston was a happier place for me because of their friendship. In 2014 and 2015, I was lucky to be hosted by friends who welcomed me into their homes as informal writing retreats. To the Davidsons in Harlem and to Brian Crabtree and Kelli Cain in Delhi, my heartfelt thanks for your hospitality (and bourbon!).

Finally, the greatest gift that Boston could ever give me was a chance encounter with Ben Merriman. From this serendipitous meeting grew a friendship that has made my life (not to mention my writing) better. I am profoundly grateful to Ben for his love, loyalty, and ability to push my thinking in new ways. For these reasons and more, Ben, I adore you.

1 Introduction

No technology is single use. Whether from hapless accident or deliberate tinkering, technology is always subject to forms of appropriation and play, misuse and reuse, often in ways that are unintended and unimagined by designers and inventors. This includes the Internet. Typically, narratives surrounding digital technologies include the military and Silicon Valley, elite knowledge workers and cutting-edge innovators. We tend not to think about bulletin board service (BBS) hobbyists (Driscoll 2014) or spammers (Brunton 2013), even though their experiments and communities were just as crucial to Internet development as efforts from college dropouts turned tech entrepreneurs. As technologies develop, dominant narratives and prescribed uses stabilize and take hold, promoting some people and uses while excluding others, and it is usually difficult to tell at the outset which practices will win out as "normal" and which will fade into obscurity.

Major players in the tech industry often share some key views about the devices and infrastructures at the root of their success and wealth: sharing is good, privacy is outdated, and technological development and corporate profit go hand in hand. As the web has become increasingly integrated into everyday communication, so has the reach of these narratives expanded, promoted by designers, users, and journalists who are looking to explain (and sell) technologies to themselves as much as each other. As a result, we associate digital technological innovation with revolutionizing workplace efficiency or the latest killer app. But there are other, less common stories of the Internet that we can tell, with different visions of how and by whom the Internet can be used.

For example, we think of social media as starting with Facebook, with roots in Ivy League universities and tech start-up culture. Yet long before Facebook was even a twinkle in a venture capitalist's eye, an international collection of body modification enthusiasts had developed their own social media platform, which eventually included blogs, a wiki, online dating apps, pod casts, and tens of thousands of images and descriptions of piercings and tattoos. Their community was small but vibrant, foreshadowing many now familiar media practices, as well as many of the tensions around how to sustain a sense of community online.

People stereotype teens and college students as being beholden to their mobile devices and addicted to Facebook updates and Twitter newsfeeds. But what about a local punk community that develops a careful network of communication technologies—both analogue and digital—to manage information about an underground network of music shows? Secrecy and flexibility are crucial to allowing this do-it-yourself (DIY) community to maintain control over protecting its scene from unwanted attention, particularly from the police. Moreover, relationships to technology in this community buck the stereotype of young people as hyperindividualized and committed to a share-everything ethic of online communication.

Social networking sites have long been used as tools of self-promotion in business contexts, which is why we plead with young people not to risk future employment opportunities by posting pictures of late-night partying. Yet these same functions of self-promotion and networking are deeply appreciated by members of Brooklyn's drag queen community, many of whom are intensely businesslike in the ways that they manage their online reputation and image. Despite the fact that transgressive gender performers might seem outside the scope of mainstream social media, for Brooklyn drag queens, Facebook and Instagram are as necessary as wigs, heels, and lipstick.

This book offers alternative narratives of increasingly common technologies as a way of expanding our ideas about who uses the Internet and how countercultural communities develop practices that help them to sustain their group ethics and identities. By looking at countercultural experiences with digital technologies, I compare the imagined uses of the web to the lived and often messy practicalities, explore how experiences of otherness shape uses of and relationships to technology, and investigate the roles that are played by social media platforms in fostering (or fragmenting) community. I introduce three field sites—a social media platform for body modification enthusiasts called *Body Modification Ezine* (BME), an underground punk rock scene in New Brunswick, New Jersey, and a growing drag community in Brooklyn, New York. Each of these communities has its own history, norms, values, and sociotechnical practices. In addition, each community sees itself as alternative, meaning that they seem themselves as challenging mainstream norms and values in some way. This sense of being alternative is important for community identity and also shapes their uses of and relationships to technology. By looking across these groups and seeing the similarities and differences that emerge, I craft an alternative set of narratives for the Internet as a tool of communication and community.

Rather than replacing popular tropes about the Internet and the ways that it came to be, I want to complicate them and perhaps call certain parts of them into question. I work from the margins as a way of evaluating many of the promises that came with the mass adoption of online technologies—that differences would be erased, tolerance would be fostered, distances of time and space would collapse, and technological innovations needed to be profitable. Drawing on extended fieldwork in three different field sites, I offer grounded, holistic accounts of how communities of outsiders have made the Internet meet their needs, developed tricks and tactics to establish and support social ties, and sometimes worked against established norms of how digital technologies should be used. On the one hand, I want to make everyday uses of the Internet appear strange and unfamiliar from the vantage point of the mainstream. At the same time, by situating these practices in the local norms and needs of countercultural users, I hope to show how the dilemmas and motivations behind these practices are nonetheless familiar.

For example, a drag queen who splits her Facebook profile into two—maintaining separate accounts for queen and boy, night and day, onstage and offstage—may produce a jarring contrast of identity. How can the same person present vastly different presentations of self, with a dramatic split of appearance, mannerisms, and language? Yet before jumping too quickly to see these practices as exceptional, the motivation is likely familiar to anyone who spends a significant amount of time online. Who hasn't experienced a moment of frustration when a distant relative comments on a Facebook update about a recent date, when a coworker sends a work-related email to a personal account, or when a new acquaintance inadvertently finds a deeply idiosyncratic Twitter feed? These mismatches of content and audience are endemic to the flattened audiences of social media. Seen in this light, when drag queens separate their Facebook accounts into two, they are simply enacting a more dramatic version of a coping strategy that many Internet users have developed to manage the complexities of everyday online life. This movement between the unfamiliar and the familiar, from the margins to the center and back again, is how I show the diversity of online practices. Further, by looking at how online technologies play a role in the lives of outsiders, I open up an analysis of the technological distributions of power.

In science and technology studies (STS), scholars have long argued that some groups tend to benefit from or be left out of dominant narratives (and markets) of technological production. Sometimes these ideologies coalesce around privilege. Ron Eglash, Jennifer L. Croissant, Giovanna Di Chiro, and Rayvon Fouché (2004, iv) have pointed out that first-world consumers fail to recognize the extent to which technology is designed for them. At other times, the design disconnect is around gender. Judy Wacjman (2004, 27) has written on the sexism of technological production, asserting that "machinery is literally designed by men with men in mind—the masculinity of technology becomes embedded in the technology itself." Mainstream heteronormative values are baked into the design of tools and technologies, and appropriations encompass the practices and adaptations that reclaim, rework, or subvert original designs.

What has always interested me about technology and what keeps me looking at the world through a technological lens is the continual conflict between the intended versus actual uses of any given tool, device, or platform—the origin myth versus the continually revised realities. In the gaps between design and use, center and margins, it becomes possible to see ideological tensions that are otherwise largely invisible, making it easier to identify and address inequalities of access and privilege. By building conversations about online life around countercultural communities, we can learn about both alterity and technology, where distinct practices and experiences of otherness underscore the richness and complexity of the tools and platforms that we use in everyday life. Looking at countercultural appropriation provides a way of identifying (and critiquing) mainstream narratives and their underlying structures of power. As Geoffrey C. Bowker and Susan Leigh Star (1999, 307) write in their influential book on the politics of infrastructure, acts of appropriation can be seen as "heralds of other worlds and of a wildness that can offset our naturalizations in libratory ways." I find countercultural practices and perspectives useful precisely as heralds of other worlds that can disrupt normative technological narratives.

Part of my interest in digital technology has to do with its centrality in how we talk about postindustrial life. Work, school, religion, politics, home life: all of these domains have been reshaped by digital code (Kitchin and Dodge 2011), and part of that reshaping extends beyond the purely technical to the social, cultural, and political. Digital technologies are simultaneously burdened by and credited with generating wealth as well as income inequality, with facilitating education through online learning and distracting students from learning, and with fostering matchmaking as well as adultery. As STS scholars have noted, the dynamic of cultural anxieties that are manifesting through narratives of technology is not unique to the Internet (Malin 2014; Marvin 1988). This tendency to let technology bear the weight of larger debates makes a cultural studies analysis of digital technology a rich area of research.

I am particularly interested in relationships between digital media and community. I argue that digital technologies alternately help and hurt the work of building community. The Internet has allowed people, particularly people at the margins, to form powerful social connections in ways that would have been impossible or at least very difficult with older modes of communication. Even as communities form through sustained online communication tools, however, they also can be upended and disrupted. In the different field sites that I have investigated, people struggle to make technology meet their needs, and community trial-and-error tactics provide important insights into a broader set of users. I consider what is lost when site administrators succumb to the pressures of constantly upgrading site features. I examine the use of technology in keeping secrets, which often doubles as a means of facilitating social exclusion. And I look at the ways that being a misfit can alternately ostracize and offer a tool for political action.

The term *community* is an elusive one, in that many people have powerful associations attached to being part of a community and yet struggle to define what separates a community from a group, family, neighborhood, or place of employment. Beyond the term's fuzziness, Miranda Joseph (2002) argues that community tends to be romanticized as an unambiguously desirable social goal, with connotations of anticapitalist (or at least nonmonetary) ethics of social connection and familylike bonds that emerge outside the home. By looking at different self-described communities (including cultural, activist, and political organizations), Joseph's work provides an important note of caution for thinking of how and when the word *community* gets deployed, arguing that the concept is sometimes used to legitimate hierarchies of gender, race, class, and sexuality.

Although I am mindful of how the word *community* can be used vaguely or irresponsibly, I still rely on the term to talk about the groups of people who are described in this book.[1] My approach has been to ask the people I interview for their preferred terms for describing the groups to which they belong and then to unpack the different meanings and values that are associated with those preferred terms. Participants in all three field studies overwhelmingly preferred the word *community*, particularly in contrast to the word *subculture*, which in common speech has negative connotations of criminality. In cultural studies, *subculture* often is used to refer to any group of people who have practices that are outside (but not necessarily in opposition to) the mainstream. In this definition, subcultures can refer to college fraternities and bowling leagues as much as fetish clubs and animal rights activists. The word *counterculture*, in contrast, has been used to refer to subcultures that intentionally oppose mainstream norms and values.[2] The groups that I study are countercultural, consciously challenging dominant paradigms of body aesthetics, economics of cultural production, and sexuality (among other things), and this sense of being in opposition to mainstream norms acts as an organizing principle for the groups that I have studied.

Another reason for working with the word *community* is to put this book into conversation with other investigations of social connection in the context of the Internet as a communication platform. All communication technologies, including the Internet, have shouldered social anxieties, and one of those anxieties has to do with the durability of community. In the 1990s, academics and industry professionals already were arguing over utopian versus dystopian visions of the Internet.[3] The optimistic view tended to see online technologies as helping people come together by rending distances and differences as almost inconsequential compared to older devices like phones. For tech utopians, the Internet promised to collapse distance and increase tolerance, which would strengthen existing communities and allow new ones to form. More pessimistic thinkers saw the Internet as a threat to existing social ties—a tool that would loosen individuals' grip on reality by substituting a superficial, virtual world. Both views can be found in the countercultural communities that I have investigated, and although I cannot resolve the debate between tech utopians and dystopians, I can lend thick descriptions and ethnographic analysis to how digital technologies shape social ties within these communities.

One way to manage the murkiness of the word *community* is to be precise about the different ways that communities are organized. There are communities of practice (Wenger 1998), where people are bound by a shared set of knowledge about doing something, often but not always tied to a job (such as accountants, travel agents, gardeners); communities of geography, where people share a collective sense of identity that stems from shared geography (neighborhoods are probably the best example); and communities of alterity, where people are bound together by shared conditions of otherness. These shared conditions of otherness not only are descriptive (meaning that demographic factors are held in common) but also are prescriptive (meaning that these conditions shape how technologies and other things are used and talked about within a community of alterity).[4]

The boundaries between these categories of community are neither fixed nor exclusive, and throughout the analysis that follows, I sometimes pull out threads that emerge less because of alterity and more because of geography and practice. For example, geography is a vital component in understanding New Brunswick's basement scene, which is deeply tied to its spatial proximity to Philadelphia and New York. Geography is also deeply important in Brooklyn's drag community, which emerged in the midst of (and is tied to) processes of urban gentrification. Drag queens also constitute a community of practice, and many of the tactics that they have developed for managing their online lives are driven by norms of drag as a profession and as a source of stigmatized sexuality. The primary framework that I use in this book, however, is of alterity.

The word *alterity* means the state of being alien or unrecognizable to the mainstream. I turn more fully to the relationship between technology and alterity in the next chapter. For now, I want to establish how I think about alterity and otherness in this book. For anthropologist Mary Douglas (1991), constructs of contaminants and messiness do not conform to social conventions of order. Using the metaphor of dirt, Douglas (1984, 35) writes that "where there is dirt there is system. Dirt is the byproduct of a systematic ordering and classification of matter, in so far as ordering involves rejecting inappropriate elements." In the context of social interactions, dirt and cleanness provide apt metaphors for understanding violations of norms and expected behavior. I find Douglas's work particularly compelling in its descriptions of the stakes for those who are conventional in stigmatizing and marginalizing those who are deeply unconventional and in its articulation of the underlying social causes for maintaining boundaries between the two.

Alterity is disruptive and can take the shape of behaving strangely or simply being a stranger. For Sara Ahmed (2000), the label of stranger is applied to any representation of otherness, where differences between strangers are often collapsed to assemble a simpler, more cohesive understanding of threat. The stranger is a relational construct that allows natives to define themselves as belonging and being at home through a process of identifying and removing those who do not belong. This conceptual process has parallels to the way that some queer theorists and activists have argued that the word *queer* is less about a discrete set of sexual desires (namely, same-sex partnerships) than about whatever practices oppose heteronormative ones (Halperin 1997).

Alterity emerges partly from what someone does (in opposition to the normal) and partly from how that behavior is read and acted on by others. A certain type of extreme body modification makes this distinction clear. I have interviewed people who have implants—silicone shapes such as stars, X's, or spheres—inserted below the skin, typically in the forearms, the back of the hands, or the forehead. These modifications are far less risky to one's health than many cosmetic surgery implants that use the same material (silicone), but they are read as marginal or even grotesque because they do not conform to standard notions of beautiful, desirable bodies. Whatever judgments are typically levied at those who opt for cosmetic surgery (such as being vain and superficial), they rarely include ostracizing, discrimination, and fear, all of which were frequently reported in my interviews with people who have obtained extreme forms of body modification. Alterity here is partly about doing something unusual to one's body and partly about interpreting what that behavior reveals and confronts about normality.

Methodological challenges come with studying alterity. In anthropology, gender studies, sociology, and human-computer interaction (HCI), there has been a tendency to fetishize otherness by celebrating outsider status at the risk of essentializing the people being studied. In other words, by focusing from the outset on marginalized status, researchers can overemphasize conditions of otherness and fail to recognize the many layers of alterity within a community as well as the many other communities (some of which may be mainstream) to which people belong.[5] Using body modification as an example, experiences of stigma can vary wildly between someone who has tattoos that can be easily hidden (such as tattoos on the back or upper arms) and someone who has substantial facial modifications (such as a lip plate or silicone implants inserted in the forehead). The more heavily modified person may receive higher status and privilege within the body modification community but the reverse among nonmodified folks in everyday locations like the grocery store. And yet if the heavily modified person has a job where colleagues accept modifications, such as a video game developer, experiences of stigma can be far less than if a high school girl from a deeply conservative family has "only" a tongue ring. Status and stigma can fluctuate wildly and be read and assessed differently within a single community and in other social settings. I do my best to avoid essentializing otherness, inspired by a "life in the round" approach (Chatman 1999; Jaeger and Burnett 2010) that tries to craft a holistic and complex account of the many trajectories and narratives within each community, the ways that those trajectories change over time, and the relationships between different facets of community members' lives.

Another complication of thinking about alterity is that on one level, everyone can be seen as occupying a position of otherness. Whether through idiosyncrasies, quirks, or even allergies (Star 1990), no one is completely normal all the time. A broad definition of *alterity* is useful for reflecting on positions of power and powerlessness in that it becomes clear that privilege and status fluctuate as people move through different communities and social contexts. Yet dwelling too long on the fact that "we are all marginal in some regard" (Star 1990, 52) risks collapsing differences between positions of alterity. I use the word *alterity* to describe distinct experiences of being on the margins, where these communities differ in important ways in different experiences and relationships to otherness. Linking this definition with my earlier descriptions of counterculture and community, throughout the book, I use the term *countercultural communities* to describe groups of people and practices and the word *alterity* to describe the conditions and relationships that give rise to those practices.

The word *practice* has a particular history in Internet studies, particularly with scholars like Henry Jenkins (2006) and Nick Couldry (2004). Here I talk about practices and tactics by drawing on the work of Michel de Certeau (1984). Although de Certeau is not explicitly a philosopher of technology, many cultural theorists and sociologists have drawn on his writings to analyze sociotechnical practices of cultural production, such as mashups (Jenkins 2013; for a countering perspective, see Manovich 2009), interpretive reading (Rothbauer 2005), and activist media (Barassi 2015). Of these examples, my approach most closely resembles Veronica Barassi's, who uses ethnographic methods to compare media practices among three groups of activists. I am similarly interested in de Certeau's understanding of how everyday life contains moments of improvisation, shortcuts, and hacks—divergences from the planned norms of prescribed routes and patterns.

Charged with the task of explaining countercultural ideology in France, in 1974 de Certeau gathered a group of thinkers who spent years conducting ethnographic research on the everyday lives of Parisians, which eventually was published as the two-volume *The Practice of Everyday Life*. De Certeau's core question centers on understanding how people maintain a sense of self in the midst of larger cultural institutions, which he views as forces that wear down and homogenize individuality. De Certeau refers to the ways that these large institutions operate as strategies, meaning that their actions are undertaken in cultural productions and political endeavors. Tactics, in contrast, are the individual shortcuts, improvisations, and workarounds that individuals use to make everyday life easier or more joyous.

As an example, more than once while conducting interviews in Brooklyn's drag community, I met queens who had changed the location of their Facebook pages to Indonesia, where it is common to have one name rather than first and last names. Although this meant that anytime they logged on to Facebook, they encountered an interface in a language they could not read, it was a reasonable trade-off for queens with a one-word stage name. This tactic allowed performers to circumvent Facebook's rules requiring first and last names, illustrating the way that everyday practices can reveal ideologies that are embedded into technological design—in this case, a bias toward Western naming conventions that was built into Facebook's terms of service.

As a concept, tactics do not require an overt political objective—they just need the intention to maneuver around or through institutional strategies. Looking at countercultural practices through a tactical framework, it is often more useful to concentrate on what tactics reveal about the strategies in which they operate. This approach is familiar to STS scholars who are interested in the politics of technology, as Langdon Winner (1986, 25) explains:

> It is obvious that technologies can be used in ways that enhance the power, authority, and privilege of some over others ... but we usually do not stop to inquire whether a given device might have been designed and built in such a way that it produces a set of consequences logically and temporally prior to any professed uses.

In my descriptions of the sociotechnical practices of different groups of outsiders, I refer to tactics as a way of identifying how interactions with technology can reveal these embedded logics and eventual consequences. As concepts, strategies and tactics appeal to me because they account for both entrenched systems of power and operations of resistance. Yet if we want to understand the Internet in a complex and holistic way, it is too limiting to create a simple binary where the empowered are strategic and the disempowered are tactical. For example, in circumstances of socioeconomic disruption, institutions of power can adapt quickly and improvisationally in ways that at first are (or seem) tactical,[6] in that they maneuver through existing infrastructure. Although these tactics eventually tend to be enfolded into (and thus reinforce) existing structures, assuming that people in power always and only operate strategically results in a narrow and flawed understanding of privilege.

If institutions can act tactically, so too can marginalized individuals act strategically. Within the small world (Chatman 1991) of a countercultural community, people may reproduce dominant strategies within their social relationships. Much to the dismay and frustration of people who are attracted to countercultures as an alternative to the power inequalities in mainstream cultures, marginalized communities commonly replicate many of the mechanisms of prejudice. When I first encountered BME, I was excited to have found a group of people who were committed to alternative ideals of bodily aesthetics, as opposed to the cookie-cutter norms of being thin, tan, and blond—norms that dominated pop culture images of femininity in my youth. Now it strikes me as naive, but I was surprised and disappointed when, at an event early in my involvement with this community, I heard a longtime BME member tell his loving, kind, and heavily tattooed wife that he would divorce her immediately if she gained weight. The obvious conflict here is that commitment to one kind of alterity in no way means that someone is free from other kinds of prejudice, like an intolerance of certain body types.

A third and perhaps more insidious example of the interweaving between weak and strong, tactical and strategic, occurs when institutions appropriate tactics into strategies and those at the center adopt and exploit practices from the margins. There are many examples of this kind of appropriation, from clothing and fashion (Fiske 1995) to workplace short cuts that are routinized into mandated routines (generally referred to as Taylorism). Although countercultural communities tend to be suspicious of having their practices (and identities) coopted by mainstream culture, a fuller accounting of the political efficacy of tactics requires thinking through a trajectory from the margins to the center and (perhaps) back again. One way of framing this book is to think of it as a de Certeauian investigation of the practices of everyday Internet life. Like de Certeau, I am interested in how people maintain a sense of agency and identity in the midst of powerful institutional forces that are invested in normative behavior (and consumption). My twists on de Certeau's approach are to focus on communities rather than individuals, alterity rather than the ordinary, and online rather than street-based practices.

Investigating Uncommon People: A Qualitative Approach

Up to this point, I have described what I want this book to do and why I think it matters. Now I want to explain how I have studied communities on the margins and their relationships to digital technologies. I take a constructionist view of social phenomena, meaning that I believe it is my job as a social scientist to gather and analyze the narratives that make up everyday life and to help us to make sense of ourselves, each other, our surroundings, and our societies (Talja, Tuominen, and Savolainen 2005). I see qualitative interviews as a way of accessing these narratives, especially when they are organized around a particular phenomenon—in this case, the roles played by online technologies in building and maintaining community. This relationship of interviewer and interviewed is neither a one-sided process (a neutral interviewer who pulls out pure strands of truth from participants) nor an even exchange of information (a tit-for-tat conversation between people with identical objectives) but rather a dynamic, co-constructed dialogue that is shaped by my interests as a researcher, participants' experiences with what I am studying, and their expectations of what an interview should be.

Interviews form the bulk of evidence in this book. I conducted interviews with members of the online body modification community in summer 2011, with a number of follow-up interviews in 2014 and 2015. Between fall 2009 and spring 2011, I was part of a research team that conducted interviews and led a focus group with members of the underground music scene in New Brunswick. Interviewees' experiences with the scene ranged from the 1990s to the present. In fall 2015, my collaborator, Adam Golub, and I conducted a series of focus groups with performers in Brooklyn's drag community and held a workshop with both performers and nightlife goers about the role played by social media in drag culture, and we held a small number of follow-up interviews in fall 2015.

I call my approach *networked field studies*, meaning that several studies are linked by a shared interest in addressing a particular set of questions. The term *networked field studies* has resonances with *case studies* (Denzin and Lincoln 2000; Travers 2001) and *multisite ethnography* (Marcus 1995), where inquiry into a given phenomenon requires moving across multiple field sites. My research requires similar mobility in terms of investigating separate communities and technologies and also in accounting for both online and offline practices. The field studies that comprise this book differ in that some used individual interviews while others used focus groups, but they are linked by an overarching thread of understanding what happens to alterity when it moves online.

A networked field studies approach combines the ethnographic connotations of fieldwork with Internet studies literature on networks (Papacharissi 2011). Partly I want to lay claim to qualitative methods that provide rich, interpretive understandings of everyday life but are not ethnography, and partly I want a term that accounts for researching across online communities and analytically drawing out shared practices and tactics. Although there have been qualitative analyses of online alterity (e.g., Hamer 2003; Hodkinson 2002; Loutzenheiser 2007; Moore 2005), these projects tend to concentrate on a single community rather than work across multiple communities or platforms. Looking at multiple countercultural communities is useful for understanding the complexities of both online technologies and marginality. Put another way, a networked field study approach accounts for multiple communities as well as multiple tools of technological connection.

Any research project with more than one field study is in some way networked because analysis works across multiple cases to develop claims and build links between data points. I use the term *networked* partly because I draw on multiple cases and partly because I want to underscore the role played by online technologies in my analysis. Regarding the latter, my approach here echoes Beth Coleman's (2011, 12) description of networked media:

> I use the term *networked media* to describe technologies that are connected to a distributed transmission network such as the Internet or cell towers. In such a case, *networked* speaks to a technical affordance. However, I also use the term to invoke a cultural sense of connectivity with one another.

Like Coleman, I use the word *networked* to refer to technological affordances and practices and also to highlight my approach to looking at these practices within the context of larger networks of people and technologies. *Networked,* then, refers both to the topic (technology) and the theoretical approach (viewing people and technologies as assemblages that bear analytical unpacking).

My use of the term *field studies* is fairly straightforward, although the term has been contested in social science research. As Christine Hine (2015, 58–59) argues, "although we routinely speak of 'the field site' in the singular, the object of study in ethnographic tradition has, in practice, rarely been a tightly bound geographic space or cultural unit." Instead, field sites tend to expand and contract over the course of a project and are always connected to other sites, institutions, and communities. Moreover, my understanding of the field has been shaped by ethnographers who seek to be similarly expansive in their concept of the field—from George Marcus's (1995) multisite ethnography to Jenna Burrell's (2012) work on thinking of field sites as nodes in a larger social technical network.

A final characteristic of the word *field* as I treat it in this work is an emphasis on the everyday. Largely this is due to influences of de Certeau, whose research concentrates on the everyday and the ordinary. And like others who study digital culture and production, I agree that "it is the quotidian experience of media, not the avant garde or exceptionally expensive, that speaks to what we actually do with media and best forecast the future of mediated worlds" (Coleman 2011, 71). Although the communities that I have studied are in many ways exceptional and avant-garde, the platforms and technologies that they use are mundane. My understanding of the field comprises both online and offline contexts, with a concentration on the everyday rather than the extraordinary.

I see two key advantages in using networked field studies as a method. First, by taking a broad view of technology and investigating sociotechnical practices as embedded in everyday life, network field studies moves us beyond a simple online or offline binary. As more and more people access the Internet via mobile phones rather than desktop computers, the division between online and offline as a meaningful way of categorizing online activity becomes increasingly tenuous (Baym 2015). Using networked field studies involves working across multiple sociotechnical assemblages within a particular community and also looking across these communities to see shared practices. As a method, the use of networked field studies lends itself to multiplicity, both in terms of multiple communities and the many different technologies and platforms that matter in the everyday lives of users and communities. Looking at digital technologies in this way gets past the reductive online or offline binary so that we can instead think about entwined fabrics of technologies and people.

Second, using networked field studies allows for analysis that works across multiple case studies. Within the context of countercultural groups, researchers have tended to look within rather than between communities (e.g., Hodkinson 2002; Nardi 2010). Using networked field studies provides a framework for thinking about conceptual links that emerge across distinct field sites. This comparative work is key for building analytical claims that extend beyond a single field site. Note that I am not making an argument about network field studies as yielding more generalizable knowledge, largely because I view generalizability as an inappropriate aim of interpretive work. Instead, I see transferability as being better suited to interpretive work. Where generalizability is about scaling up, transferability is about moving between—tracing connections between field sites rather than generalizing or making universal claims. Transferability is baked into networked field studies as a method because the comparative analysis seeks to identify practices and characteristics that emerge across distinct communities and sites.

Although my work is qualitative, I would not call it ethnography. I did not spend sustained periods of time living with these communities as part of my research process. I use the word *ethnographic* throughout as a nod to the participant observation that was conducted at each field site. During fieldwork, I attended basement shows in New Brunswick and drag shows in Brooklyn. I have been a member of BME for over a decade, and while conducting interviews for the research in this book, I hung out in tattoo and piercing shops and attended community events like barbecues and campouts. Meeting people, attending events, and taking copious notes helped me to situate material from interviews in a wider context of community norms and values. In this sense, I am inspired by and rely on tools of ethnography without necessarily meeting the standards for traditional definitions of this method, online or off.[7]

Another methodological note before moving on: it always is important for researchers to minimize any negative consequences that could result for participants who are involved in a research project, but this obligation is even more vital when studying groups that are in some way marginalized or disenfranchised. The arguments and analysis that are at the core of this book come from a willingness on behalf of countercultural community members to share narratives of their lives and technological practices, which risks exposing their community to increased scrutiny, whether from authorities or from curious but potentially problematic onlookers. In addition to using pseudonyms to protect the confidentiality of participants, I have sought feedback from different stakeholders at each site about how much information to disclose about the sites (both physical and digital) and practices described in this book. I expand at length on my methodological process in the appendix, including a detailed discussion of my approach to ensuring ethical engagement with these communities.

Chapter Outline

Following this introductory chapter, I discuss in chapter 2 the dominant narratives that surround online technologies and outline the various problems and inequalities that the Internet allegedly is poised to solve. As is mentioned above, these promises emerged from designers of technology, from users, and from the academics and journalists who are charged with mediating between those two groups. By laying out these issues, I set up popular framings of online technologies and contrast them with the experiences of the countercultural communities that I investigate. Put another way, to identify sociocultural tactics, it is first necessary to understand the strategies in which they operate. I see this chapter as addressing technologies as they are designed and described strategically so that I can then turn to an analysis of countercultural tactics that emerge within and between. A second focus of chapter 2 is to give an account of technology and alterity. Reviewing research from STS, media archeology, and Internet studies, I build a list of key themes that emerge from technologies that come from and are built for the margins, including legibility (technologies that are created in ways that allow community members to track and adjudicate changes over time), flexibility (technologies that lend themselves to tactical practices of improvisation and change), and authenticity (technologies that reflect countercultural ideologies). Identifying these qualities helps improve consistency in my analysis of the sociotechnical practices that emerged from the networked field studies that comprise the following chapters.

In chapter 3, I introduce *Body Modification Ezine* (BME), focusing on how members of this group of body modification enthusiasts have dealt with maintaining community boundaries and a sense of alterity over the course of BME's twenty-year history online. For many members of this community, the Internet at first offered a powerful means of connecting with others with shared interests, sharing information, and building a sense of community. As more and more people went online and social media became increasingly popular, however, information that had long been hidden became easier and easier to find, threatening BME's exclusivity through increased attention to and commodification of body modification. Chapter 3 focuses on the politics of insiders and outsiders by looking at tensions that emerge when both the technological and cultural practices of a countercultural community become popularized. How did BME as a community make decisions about inclusivity and exclusivity? When mainstream social network sites emerged and became increasingly popular in the early 2000s, how did BME members respond? Legibility emerged as an important ethic of initially setting up policies and rules, but new challenges surfaced as both social media and body modification increased in popularity. BME's history of providing online social connectivity and information provides a trajectory for the complexities that emerge when a community struggles to include those with similar interests, exclude those with suspect motives, and maintain a sense of otherness in the face of increasing online access.

Many of these same themes of insiders and outsiders surface in chapter 4, which looks at the underground punk music community in New Brunswick, New Jersey. Punk politics and a do-it-yourself (DIY) ethic have long characterized the music scene in New Brunswick, which has launched successful bands such as the Bouncing Souls, Gaslight Anthem, and the Screaming Females. I look at information practices of secrecy as they emerge for members of this community, who strive to keep their activities off the radar, both figuratively and literally. The paradox here is to put information online in a way that gives other community members enough information to participate in upcoming events without revealing details of these activities to the authorities.[8] Looking at the tactics that have been developed by this this community exposes the limits of social media platforms for keeping community secrets. I use the lens of flexibility to describe the multiple tactics that have been developed to maintain the integrity of the basement community. Looking at norms of secrecy and shifting from the individual notion of privacy to the collective practices of secrecy can provide a new perspective on collective tactics for controlling information in the context of surveillance and monitoring.

In chapter 5, my final field study focuses on Brooklyn's drag community, which has blossomed into a vibrant nightlife scene. Drag queens described Facebook as vital to their work as performers, to a highly local sense of community, and to a broader sense of queer culture and identity. At the same time, participants were deeply critical of Facebook as a platform that failed to accommodate the fluidity and complexity of their countercultural identities. In particular, Facebook's authentic-name policy (formerly called its real-name policy) allows me to develop a critique of authenticity as a sociotechnical characteristic that allows communities of alterity to see themselves, their norms, and their values in the technologies that they use every day. In considering how drag queens across the United States were able to develop a coalition that succeeded in forcing Facebook to apologize for and eventually rework its policies, I argue that countercultural politics alone cannot provoke a change in policy, especially when the platforms are illegible and inflexible in their policies. Working as a community of misfits, drag queens mobilized through a combination of being willing to be visible and making visible their alterity.

The themes that are drawn out from and across these field studies include membership boundaries, collective rulemaking, secrecy and privacy, alterity, and performativity. In the final chapter of this book, chapter 6, I synthesize these findings into a set of claims about how online technologies matter, both in terms of alterity and community. Returning to the dominant Internet narratives that are described in chapter 2, I argue that the contemporary push for mobility and cross-platform interoperability can work to the detriment of communities that are looking to develop a sense of place online. I also look at how countercultural relationships to digital technologies speak to battles over online anonymity and work through the advantages and disadvantages of building one's own online platforms (as body modification folks did with BME) versus making mainstream platforms work for countercultural needs (more in line with how Brooklyn drag queens use digital technologies). Working with the three-part framework of flexibility, legibility, and authenticity, I offer a guideline for design ethics or countercultural values in design, looking to shape how technologies approach building tools to support different kinds of communities.

I see my project as one that constructs a kaleidoscope of different communities and technologies, twisting and refocusing on different fragments of sociotechnical practices used in the communities that I examine as they come together and (sometimes) fall apart. The combined effect of these twists and shifts is more of a collaged assemblage than a well-defined, clear-cut image of the Internet as an object of study. Within the many practices, experiences, and struggles discussed in this text, the richness of online practices becomes glaringly, excitingly apparent. From this rich set of tactics at the margins, we gain tools for a clearer analysis of how technological artifacts embed ideologies, making it possible rethink practices and uses that have been established as normative. Ultimately, what is at stake in this book is the radical potential for addressing gaps of power and privilege through the (re)discovery of the Internet's depth, breadth, and strangeness—the ways that it enables exploration, secrecy, connection, and community.

2 Frameworks for Technology and Communities of Alterity

Technology is neither good nor bad, nor is it neutral. This dictum—known as Kranzberg's first law of technology (Kranzberg 1986)—is a good starting point for this chapter, in which I develop the analytical toolkit that draws together the three field studies that are at the core of this text. Like Melvin Kranzberg, I do not see digital technologies as inherently good or bad. Instead, I see devices and platforms as woven together in networks of people and spaces but as unevenly distributed, serving some people better than others. To think about the capacity of digital technologies to support countercultural communities, it is helpful to step away from thinking of technologies as ideologically neutral and instead to consider the contexts in which they are created and deployed.

The first goal of this chapter is to present three persistent assumptions about online technologies—that online activity relates to (dis)embodiment, that the Internet is a platform for authenticity and experimentation, and that web-based interactions are placeless. Looking at dominant claims about the use and design of online technologies allows me to show that they are nonneutral and always already laden with prioritized, legitimized uses. The same origin stories that provide a slanted and limiting framework for viewing a technology can also shape assumptions about how a given set of tools and devices should be used. My objective is to set up a clearer contrast between prevailing assumptions about online technologies and the practices of countercultural communities. I return to these strategic narratives in the book's conclusion, using analysis of fieldwork to evaluate and speak back to conventional discourses of social relationships and online technologies.

The second goal of this chapter is to develop an analytical framework for considering practices and tactics of countercultural communities.

Synthesizing scholarship from STS, communication theory, information science, and Internet studies, I develop a list of features that are important or useful for communities of alterity—*legibility* (technologies created in ways that allow community members to track and adjudicate changes over time), *flexibility* (technologies that lend themselves to tactical practices of improvisation and change), and *authenticity* (technologies that reflect countercultural ideology). Throughout this book, I return to these features to assess the tactical capacity of the sociotechnical assemblages used by people in the groups that I am analyzing, helping to build a more coherent understanding of how online technologies support the coming together of alternative communities.

Dominant Narratives of the Internet

Given how ingrained online technologies have become in everyday life, it is easy to forget the initial excitement surrounding the emergence of online tools and the enormous range of conjectures and demands that immediately arose regarding the Internet. I want to treat these genres of excitement seriously as narratives that indicate how (and for whom) the Internet has been imagined. In de Certeau's (1984) terms, the assumptions that I am outlining are strategic in that they stem from dominant, institutional framings of the Internet as a set of communication tools and socioeconomic possibilities (Chun 2006; Flichy 2007). By working through these narratives (which have received significant critical attention in Internet studies scholarship), I examine the reasons for their persistence in everyday conversations about the Internet. When we hold on to notions of the Internet as something that allows disembodied users to explore authentic selves, removed from time and place, what exactly are we holding on to? Whom do these narratives serve? What sorts of subject positions, identities, and communities drop out of these narratives?

In identifying three key themes relating to how the Internet is experienced and described in mainstream technological discourses (disembodiment, experimentation, and placelessness), followed by three characteristics for thinking about technological alterity (legibility, flexibility, and authenticity), I do not mean to set up a direct correlation between the two. Rather, the themes and characteristics that I have identified here provide two different lenses—strategic and tactical, respectively—for analyzing the relationships between countercultural communities and digital technologies. The countercultural appropriations that I discuss in the following chapters can be thought of as a tactical foil to the strategic narratives that I identify here, and I describe legibility, flexibility, and authenticity as the characteristics that support the work of building community for countercultural groups.

The Disembodiment of Online Interactions

An early and popular trope about interpersonal dynamics shaped by web-mediated interactions is that online interactions are disembodied and virtual and that offline interactions are embodied and concrete. In this narrative, people leave their bodies behind to interact online, to the point that the physical body essentially ceases to matter. This rhetoric still lingers in journalistic and (to a lesser degree) academic writing and is regularly reinforced in popular science fiction. For instance, Keanu Reeves's character Neo in *The Matrix* (1999) enters a cyberreality through a web portal and leaves behind his inert, vulnerable body in the real world. Feminist critiques have refuted assumptions about the trope of online disembodiment, objecting to the suggestion that the material body ceases to matter as soon as online activity begins (see boyd 2001; Burrell 2012; Hine 2015; Nakamura 1995, 2013; Rybas and Gajjala 2007). These writers note the impossibility of shutting off the components of our subjectivity that shape how we think, behave, and relate to others. As Shaka McGlotten (2013, 3) puts it in his book on queer men and digital media, "the fluidity and playfulness of cyberspace and the intimacies it was supposed to afford have been punctuated by corporeality." In other words, the body has a tendency to reassert itself, even when we might imagine that technology allows us to leave it behind.

To some extent, the prevalence of mobile devices can make this debate feel outdated. A clear division between online and offline is increasingly difficult to maintain in a context of mobile Internet connections and always listening home devices. When we move through the world with continual online access, a tidy on/off binary seems tenuous at best. But a subtler version of this binary persists when we assign different values to online and offline behaviors and practices. For example, hate speech and threats of violence are frequently tolerated or dismissed when made online, despite examples of online harassment leading to horrific consequences (see Gutman and Haskell 2013; Newton 2013). The logic of devaluing the seriousness of online violence is often based on an assumption that the virtual is somehow less real, a response that relies on perceiving online interactions as disembodied and removed.

As is the case in all three themes of how the Internet shapes communication and identity, rhetoric of the Internet as an agent of disembodiment cannot be dismissed entirely. Medical research has offered compelling evidence of the long-term consequences of how sustained time in front of a computer contributes to sedentary living (Harding 2010). Mobile online users are not immune from health concerns, given both the physical conditions that can result from habitual use of these devices and the number of accidents that result every year from paying attention to smartphones over, say, subway trains (Collins 2013). These physical consequences stem from being engrossed in our screens and devices to the point of ignoring or forgetting the body. A clean division between online as disembodied and abstract and offline as embodied and concrete has largely (and rightly) been dismissed, yet it persists in the devaluation of online harassment and the difficult of attending to the body while online.

Online Experimentations in Authenticity

The concept of authenticity is connected to the previous discussion of (dis) embodiment, where freedom from the constraints of the body allows for experimentation and play, which in turn let people express themselves. The implicit understanding here is that the rules and norms of social life restrict people's ability to express themselves fully in person. Online interactions, in contrast, permit people to identify in new ways and to play with presentation of self in terms of their gender, ethnicity, or sexuality. William Merrin (2007, para. 9) summarizes this set of assumptions, citing the early and influential Internet studies scholar Sherry Turkle:

> The "self" [that Turkle] valorises may well be "multiple" and "distributed" rather than a natural real-life given, but her conclusion that the online world is a space of self-expression and an aid to greater "self-knowledge," "personal transformation" and "growth" clearly indicates that for her the self is strengthened by its virtual connections.

Similar to the prior trope of online/offline as disembodied/embodied, communication and Internet scholars were quick to note the inaccuracies of Turkle's stance. For example, Lisa Nakamura's (1995, 2013) influential work on identity tourism persuasively argues that experimentation and play with different genders and races contains an inherent essentialism, "allow[ing] a player to appropriate a ... racial identity without any of the risks associated with being a racial minority in real life" (Nakamura 1995, 3). A key issue here is that a person who has experimented with a marginalized identity online might think that he fully understands the experiences and history of that identity, even if his Internet interactions were in fact fleeting or superficial.

In 2011, in a dramatic enactment of the problems and complexities of authenticity, a forty-year-old straight, white man from the United States, Tom MacMaster, was exposed as the "real" author of the blog "A Gay Girl in Damascus," which detailed everyday life as a queer woman during Syria's Arab spring (Bell and Flock 2011). In addition to duping thousands of readers, MacMaster also conducted a relationship with a woman who believed that she was involved in a long-distance, lesbian romance. Among the reasons that MacMaster cited for impersonating someone of a different race, religion, gender, and sexuality were his desire to promote political issues and his belief that it would be a more compelling, more authentic blog if he claimed to be a queer activist in Syria rather than a concerned political commenter from Georgia in the United States. MacMaster presumed that his political argument would be more persuasive if it reflected the "authentic" experience of a queer woman in the Middle East, where there's an undeniable irony in a straight, white man lamenting the difficulty of having his views heard and valued in public.

For MacMaster, the Internet provided a vehicle for identity tourism, but for many people, online tools are leveraged less sensationally for a different kind of performance, based not on an entirely different race or gender but on an idealized version of the self. A great deal of Internet studies research has concentrated on how technologies offer platforms for identity experimentation and self-promotion (Hogan 2010; Liu 2007). In her book on social media and white-collar workers, Melissa Gregg (2011, 101) ties the aspirational performativity of Facebook to its roots in an elite academic institution (Harvard University) and an enduring ethic of self-promotion: "Facebook is the latest means by which the aspiring middle class creates distinctive expressions of its own privileged position in social space. This is because the command of virtual territories is increasingly crucial to the rewards to be won in society at large." The phenomenon of self-branding via online platforms has been of particular interest to people who study celebrity (Marwick 2013), a culture in which social media are important tools for both gaining and displaying status. Whether in the context of major celebrities or ordinary office workers, the strategic link between self-promotion and the Internet highlights the extent to which our online selves are constantly performed and constructed rather than innate or natural.

In addition to self-promotion, discussions of online authenticity open up debates about anonymity and pseudonymity, which sometimes are grouped as the "nym" movement. Working against claims that online anonymity leads to (or is indicative of) cybercrime and online harassment, activist and academic thinkers aligned with the nym movement argue for the advantages of pseudonymity and anonymity for personal freedom. In online communities, however, even those who use pseudonyms can be identified through markers of behavior and idiosyncrasies of interaction.[1] As Celia Pearce (Pearce and Artemesia 2009, 140) notes in her account of an online gamer, "while the person's real-life identity remains anonymous, her in-world identity, because it is persistent, cannot stay that way for long. Over time, others will recognize the traits and talents of the individual, often before she recognizes them herself." In this case, authenticity emerges as a durable set of practices and behaviors that can resist an individual's attempts to manufacture new or temporary behaviors. Pearce's arguments relate to online communities because sustained, interpersonal interactions are required for the familiarity and legibility that help us identify people online based solely on behavior. In the conceptual arc that I am tracing, authenticity shifts from identity tourism to identity promotion to identity as idiosyncratic behavior. All of these understandings of authenticity take the individual as a central organizing feature, in contrast to the more collective sense of authenticity that I develop in this book and introduce at the end of this chapter.

The Internet as Collapsing Space and Time

Another common characterization of the Internet is as a tool that collapses distance and time. When content and Internet providers emphasize the speed and ease of delivering reliable and fast online connectivity, they are tapping into this rhetoric of the Internet's ability to span the distance between producers and viewers, customers and products. Although online technologies are heralded as singular and revolutionary for their ability to communicate across vast distances quickly and easily, the Internet is only the most recent technological artifact that provokes people to say that geographic distance is being rendered null and void (see Marvin 1988). Part of the reason that the notion of collapsing of space has persisted has to do with the ways that spatial metaphors proliferate in common discourses about the Internet. From web *sites* to page *visits*, our language for talking about online interactions is heavily indebted to metaphors of space. Critiques of these metaphors arose almost as quickly as the technologies themselves (e.g., Druick 1995; Harrison and Dourish 1996; Lyman 1998; Stefik 1997), but they endure in ways that have consequences for thinking about how the Internet functions in everyday life.

It is true that digital technologies enable cheap and immediate communication across vast distances, making transnational communication easy and even mundane. But sociocultural complications emerge from the use of these technologies, including concerns of privacy, social media burnout, and uneven access. Mark Graham (2013, 9) has suggested a troubling explanation for the persistence of spatial metaphors, particularly among policymakers, where "a dualistic offline/online worldview can depoliticize and mask the very real and uneven power relationships between different groups of people." In other words, the claim that communication technologies collapse distance participates in a technological determinism framework, where access to technology is assumed to remedy structural inequalities of class and privilege. And distance does matter in terms of how we use and think of online technologies, who has network accessibility, and how people behave when they are removed from social, political, or economic power. In her ethnography of Internet cafe users in Ghana, Jenna Burrell (2012) describes how access to the Internet does not, in fact, neutralize distance because the young people she interviewed often struggled to understand or adapt to Western norms of online interaction. Moreover, Burrell notes that concerns over cybercrime led to calls to segregate countries like Ghana from transnational online connections, a dramatic instance of the ways that online access is not agnostic to location.

Space is not as straightforward a concept as dominant narratives about the Internet might suggest, and neither is time. Efficiency and productivity are hallmarks of how digital technologies tend to be marketed and valued, yet these same technologies can make us feel that time is being expanded or contracted (Hassan 2007). Digital devices can make work productive, but they can intrude into our personal lives (Gregg 2011), producing a sense of constant exhaustion (Mazmanian 2015). The Internet can also impose its own sense of time. For example, people who play massively multiplayer online roleplaying games (MMORGs) usually need to coordinate efforts across several time zones (Nardi 2012). In some games, time is calibrated to servers' ability to complete tasks, meaning that time is calculated with computers' rather than people's actions as the organizing principle (Torfi Olafsson, private communication, 2016). Because digital technologies can speed up, slow down, or otherwise alter our perceptions of time, we need a much more robust account of how online communication tools shape our understanding of time than is typically on offer when we acknowledge only the rhetoric of workplace efficiency.

Readers familiar with Internet studies and computer-mediated communication scholarship might be surprised by the extent to which I have discussed tropes about the Internet that have been thoroughly batted around in scholarly debates.[2] Despite the academic attention that has been paid to the problematic rhetoric of online/offline binaries and the hollow promises that the Internet allows for authentic identity work and collapses distance, these tropes continue to carry weight. In advertisements and university classrooms, associations between digital technologies and disembodiment, authenticity, and traversing time and space are common. These promises support a powerful network of industry actors—including Internet providers, social media startups, and smartphone manufacturers—who have a vested interest in promoting claims that online resources are not just convenient but necessary and moreover are a form of self-expression. As rhetoric about the Internet as a means of identity work, self-exploration, and interpersonal connection becomes ingrained in our understanding of how these tools are meant to be used, the tools themselves become naturalized into the structures and norms of everyday life, ensuring the survival and profitability of the corporations that produce and develop digital technologies. Moreover, the normalization of communication technologies as being aligned with mainstream identities and industries forecloses other sociotechnical possibilities. The real consequences for bodies, relationships, and corporate interests all point back to Kranzberg's law, demonstrating the ideological stakes of digital technologies for both common and uncommon uses and for the prevailing logics that determine which is which.

Appropriation and Alterity

I have opted to discuss the dominant narratives that surround online platforms at length because I want to consider appropriations of and play with technologies that emphasize different values of what online tools can do and how they should be used. If rhetorical moves like disembodied Internet use, authentic online identity work, and communication tools neutralizing space give rise to the strategic norms surrounding online technologies, how can we think about their tactical potential? In other words, if disembodiment, authenticity, and placelessness inform the dominant perceptions of digital technologies, what characteristics support its radicalization? As Nelly Oudshoorn and Trevor Pinch (2005, 1) remind us, "there is no one correct use for a technology," and history is littered with examples of technologies that were designed to solve one problem and ended up being put to another use entirely.[3] In STS literature, this repurposing of technology is often referred to as appropriation.

Technologies do not emerge fully formed from an ideologically blank, ethically neutral vault but are designed, developed, tested, and marketed by real people who have their own values, prejudices, ambitions, and assumptions about what a particular artifact should do and what a given user should look like. These assumptions are rarely explicit, but they have important consequences for the success or failure of a given technology in terms of adoption and use. In each of the field studies that comprises the core of this book, I discuss the countercultural appropriations (which I also call tactics) that emerge when each community engages with online technologies. To do so consistently and to offer a framework that can be applied to other communities, I focus on three characteristics that emerged across field studies—legibility, flexibility, and authenticity.

My analysis of online technologies and communities of alterity is influenced by academics and activists who have assembled their own metrics of technological alterity. Looking at "socialized media," Robert W. Gehl (2014) argues that activist platforms should by definition and design offer four key features—two-way communication, decentralization, free and open-source software, and encryption. Gehl reconsiders how media systems should be designed in ways that protect user agency and facilitate projects of social justice but takes more of a top-down view of reworking dominant platforms than my bottom-up account of communities that rework or work around existing technologies to meet community needs. Writing as a legal theorist, Julie E. Cohen (2012, 255) suggests that a guiding ethic for sociotechnical policy should be fostering creativity and play: "to enable capabilities for human flourishing, the material and informational infrastructures of the networked information society must afford sufficient room for creative, material, and identity play." When I refer to countercultural practices as a form of play, I mean in the sense that Cohen describes—technologies that allow creativity and human flourishing, both of which resonate with the broader de Certeauian influences in my work.

Research on digital media and activism has provided another set of guidelines for thinking about the political potential of appropriating Internet technologies.[4] Todd Wolfson's (2014) history of the indymedia movement analyzes how activists use online technologies as part of what Wolfson calls the cyber left. Wolfson identifies three tenets of the cyber left, including a commitment to using new media technologies, a decentralized organizational structure, and participatory democracy as a governing principle, arguing that indymedia activists focus on creating participatory technologies rather than engaging in truly inclusive political mobilization. Sasha Costanza-Chock (2014) reviews the use of digital technologies among activists, particularly young people who were working for immigration reform in Los Angeles in the United States. Costanza-Chock notes the capacity of digital media to support do-it-yourself methods and nonmainstream content, themes that I pick up in several field studies that are discussed below. Taking a comparative approach, Veronica Barassi (2015) uses ethnographic methods to investigate how European activist communities used digital media. Barassi's account points out the advantages and drawbacks that activists assigned to online platforms as tools for political organization. Both methodologically and analytically, my approach is similar in that I work across multiple field sites to develop ideas on how digital technologies alternately support and create problems within countercultural communities.

Writing about the perceptions and uses of technology among poor and working-class women, Virginia Eubanks (2011) outlines a "high tech equity agenda" for promoting social justice in technology-related policy decisions.

Eubanks argues that any radical agenda for addressing inequalities that is related to digital tools and media must take a broad view of what constitutes the technological and be willing to engage issues of income inequality, tax loopholes for corporations, social welfare programs, barriers to democratic participation, and local legislation for land use and rent control. I share Eubanks's (2011, 156) view that any serious accounting of technological activism must extend beyond individual tools and devices because "broadening our focus beyond developing technological artifacts and skills … [opens up] a way to think more broadly about what social justice means in the information age." Although my research relates less directly to activism, I also see the technological as deeply ingrained into the spheres of politics and civic life. Across these texts on activism and online technologies, there are both opportunities for organizing and drawbacks in the project of developing and sustaining community life.

Building on the above texts, I offer my own framework for evaluating the politics of the appropriative practices that emerge in this book, in which appropriation is identified in terms of de Certeauian values such as improvisation, experimentation, and play. In the chapters that follow, I use this framework—of legibility, flexibility, and authenticity—to assess the countercultural tactics of the communities that I have investigated, identifying points of commonality and divergence.

Legibility

I use *legibility* to refer to a meaningful openness about how a platform is managed, maintained, and altered. My understanding of legibility is influenced by two different lenses on technology—the first from legal theories of privacy and design values and the second from library science theory on classification and cataloging schemes. In her treatise on contextual privacy, Helen Nissenbaum (2010) argues that one driver of the loss of privacy is the inability of everyday people to adjudicate entities that capture, store, and monetize individual data. This echoes Daniel Solove's (2011) discussion of prevalent metaphors of privacy. Rather than draw on Orwellian metaphors of totalitarian surveillance, Solove describes privacy today as Kafkaesque because information continually and bewilderingly shifts between actors, systems, and networks and people are never clear about how information is being gathered, used, or archived. For Solove, understanding threats to privacy as a civil liberty is less about totalitarian regimes that monitor citizens' movements and more about people's inability to see or contest structures of surveillance that are increasingly common in everyday life. Similarly, by comparing the Library of Congress Subject Headings (LCSH) to Google search results, Emily Drabinski (2013) argues that the lack of access to search engine algorithms leaves us unable to interrogate the categorization of information (see also Annany 2011; Pariser 2011). Drabinski notes that although the ways that particular texts are described or located within a cataloging hierarchy can be agreed with or disputed, Library of Congress documentation allows us to trace how terms have evolved over time and how terms within the LCSH hierarchy relate to each other. Both for protecting individual privacy and understanding data, legible structures of information are crucial.

Research on craft and technology has made similar arguments against a "black box" mentality that shrouds technical functionality from view (Pasquale 2015). In this line of critique, users should be able to see how technologies are put together and how they can come apart, which also can be called an ethic of transparency. Matthew B. Crawford (2009) uses the example of luxury car engines (which are occluded and inaccessible) and old motorcycle parts (which are visible and configurable). Ethics of transparency also matter on social network sites, where important information like targeted advertising and privacy guidelines is obscured through a combination of technical and legal opacity (Turow 2011). The most utilitarian definition of *legibility* might be "the ability of technology users to alter design specifications at any moment," but this level of technical skill is beyond the interests and skillsets of most social media users. I take a somewhat broader view, where *legibility* means "the ability of users to see and speak back to policies and practices of an online platform." In the context of countercultural communities and their relationships to information and communications technologies (ICTs), key questions about legibility that I ask include "What mechanisms exist to identify protocols for the use and continuity of a given platform?" and "Are there articulated rules for contesting or renegotiating these protocols?"

Flexibility

Flexibility is the ability to reconfigure technological platforms to produce new content or interactions. One approach for thinking about technological flexibility comes from mash-up culture, where people use media tools to create, rework, and distribute media content (Jenkins, Ford, and Green 2013; Sinnreich 2010). For scholars working with mash-ups and participatory media, flexibility is valuable as a means of opening up previously restricted technologies of cultural production, and in the field studies comprising this text (particularly the punk music and drag communities), producing media content is a vital part of community participation. Yet I am more interested in practices than in content, and I look at flexibility more in terms of the processes that a technology affords and less in terms of the artifacts themselves.

As an example from feminist human-computer interaction (HCI) research, Elizabeth Goodman and Janet Vertesi (2012) evaluate the design ethics that are embedded in sex toys, noting the ways in which gender and sexuality norms are manifested in devices like vibrators and web cams. They found that the devices that most reflected feminist ethics allowed a two-way dialogue of use (between designer and user) rather than a one-way relationship of use (where a user interacts with an object only as its creators initially imagined it would be used). Although they do not use the word *flexibility*, Goodman and Vertesi argue for an evaluation of sex toys in terms of users' ability to customize and reimagine them. Flexibility is also reflected in the bottom-up leadership structures that are evident in many media activist (Wolfson 2014) and gamer (Pearce and Artemesia 2009, 153) communities, which support minimally hierarchical dynamics of power that tend to arise in the absence of highly formalized leadership mechanisms. My assessment of flexibility asks about technological affordances for improvisation and play and looks to identify practices that change over time and in response to limits of larger or more mainstream structures.

Authenticity

The third component of my analytical framework is *authenticity*, or the ability of a group to see its own ethics and values in the technologies that they use in everyday life. Digital technologies are authentic when the content, policies, and design of a platform reflect users' own ideals rather than a design that defaults to heteronormative and patriarchal values. My use of the word *authentic* is narrow, largely because the term is an elusive one that often is defined relationally or in opposition to something else. As Sarah

Banet-Weiser (2012) argues in her book on self-promotion and branding, the meanings of *authenticity* have shifted over time. Romantics felt that an authentic self resides deep within, below superficial layers of sociocultural norms. For Romantics, authenticity emerges after social conventions have been peeled away, not unlike how early Internet enthusiasts viewed online experiments in identity. In Marxist discourse, authenticity is positioned in contrast to the commercial. Postindustrial Marxist ideas of human subjectivity—at least in the context of work—viewed interventions of automation as alienating, a process that leads workers to feel disconnected both from themselves and their products. There is a contradiction here between two views of technology and authenticity. In Marxist thinking, technology does not allow a true, hidden self to emerge (as early conceptualizations of the Internet proposed) but instead renders the individual less human and more robotic.

Thinking of authenticity as tied to the nonautomated was reflected by the Frankfurt school, particularly Walter Benjamin's (2008) *The Work of Art in the Age of Mechanical Reproduction* (1935); the craft movement (Crawford 2009; Sennett 2008); and the DIY movements (Ratto and Boler 2014). To the different discourses of authenticity that Banet-Weiser (2012) has identified, I add a Freudian narrative—in which an individual's self-conceptualization involves a confrontation of personal desires with social norms, and authenticity accounts for those desires within a larger trajectory of psychological development. In a Freudian understanding, talking through personal desires and drives results in an authentic understanding of the self.

There is a tendency in these definitions to think of authenticity as fundamentally individual—as something that people attain for or reveal about their inner self. But communities can also develop a sense of authenticity, meaning a shared set of ideas about who they are and what matters to them. Grafting this collective understanding of authenticity onto technology, *authenticity* refers to the capacity of a tool or platform to reflect local ethics and values. Locality is important here as a way of avoiding the abstraction and slipperiness of defining *authenticity*. Tying authenticity to concrete and specific values helps ground this characteristic as a manifestation of a specific community and their ethics. When I refer to a technology as authentic, I privilege the collective over the individual and emphasize the local over the nameless and general.

In developing these characteristics as a framework for thinking about technological alterity, I do not want to imply a rigid checklist of design values or suggest that each value is necessarily present when a countercultural community uses digital technologies, nor do I support determinist arguments by implying that technologies with these features will cause countercultures to flourish and communities to thrive. I see technology and everyday practices as mutually constitutive, taking shape against and through each other. I also see communities as complex, sometimes contradictory social arrangements that are subject to change over time. In the field studies that follow, I identify practices and tactics that help define these characteristics in a grounded way, using thick descriptions of the everyday uses of digital technologies, but I also note when legibility, flexibility, and authenticity are lacking.

Beyond establishing a vocabulary for how I have come to think about digital technologies in the context of countercultural technologies, I see the framework of legibility, flexibility, and authenticity as a crucial binding agent in a comparative discussion of field studies. As a method, networked field studies involves investigating multiple communities and looking at practices that emerge across them, where they converge and diverge. Acknowledging that all technologies, including online tools, are not neutral is necessary but not sufficient for identifying the ideologies that are woven into digital platforms and the ways that those ideologies matter for people who use those tools from day to day. That work of identification and analysis requires a framework with well-articulated components—in this case, legibility, flexibility, and authenticity. Together, these concepts allow me to analyze cohesively and consistently the different efforts, successes, and failures of countercultural groups that use digital technologies as part of the everyday work of building, managing, and sustaining community.

3 The Death and Life of Great Online Subcultures: An Analysis of *Body Modification Ezine*

In 1994, ten years before Harvard University students were sending the first Facebook friend requests, an international group of body modification enthusiasts had come together on the social media site *Body Modification Ezine* (BME). Founded by a former online casino designer, BME was an early adopter of many now-familiar Internet trends, including personal blogging, online dating, podcasts, and wikis. The site focused on different forms of body modification, including tattoos, piercings, and rarer and more extreme forms of altering the body, such as suspensions and flesh pulls, scarification, corseting, extreme genital modifications, ear pointing, tongue splitting, and the voluntary amputation of digits, limbs, and organs. BME's history provides a useful window into the enormous range of bodily practices that have emerged as forms of personal, cultural, and political expression and a record of a community driven far beyond common forms of cosmetic alteration.[1] But the site is also an entry point to thinking about technology, community, and alterity.

From the start, BME positioned itself as an online haven for outsiders, a message that it continues to promote in its statement of purpose:

> We are an uncommon subculture and community built by and for modified people. We are the historians, practitioners and appreciators of body modification. We are the collaborative and comprehensive resource for the freedom of individuality in thought, expression and aesthetic. We serve you and ourselves as a source of inspiration, entertainment and community.

I am interested in what this statement claims and what it leaves out, what BME has achieved as an online counterculture and also how it has faltered. Recalling Mary Douglas's (1991) distinction between dirt and order, I want to account for what BME disrupted with its emergence as well as what has counted as disruption within BME as a countercultural community.

I also am interested in when and how disruption surfaced between BME and other emergent social media platforms, introducing a competition for attention, participation, and the production of content. What tactics did BME develop to build and sustain itself as a countercultural community? What sources of tension emerged to work against the site's stability and survival? A close look at BME's norms, design values, practices, and tactics reveals a complex account of key concerns for any community of alterity—determining insiders and outsiders, developing rules of behavior, and protecting a sense of otherness. As a community, BME developed rules and politics for managing different tensions and disruptions among its users, where legibility emerged as a key tenet in many decisions and approaches. Although it is not a truly democratic platform, many of BME's membership policies show a commitment to highly legible processes for dealing with problematic users and behaviors. Yet a legible set of rules was ultimately inadequate for the community's survival as new and more mainstream social media platforms competed for attention and content.

I first encountered BME in high school while searching for information on piercings and scarification. A few years later, I was a member who logged in regularly, participated in forum discussions, reviewed content for the site, and made lasting social ties. I have a number of modifications, including piercings, tattoos, stretched ears, and scarifications. I also have engaged in suspensions and flesh pulls, attended tattoo and scarification conventions, and been featured on tattoo blogs. Despite these experiences and friendships, I would describe my relationship to the body modification community as tangential. In fact, the closest friendships that I made through BME were with people who were critical of others in the modified community. Among these more critical perceptions, modified folks were described as shallow, overly socially exclusive, and eager to play games of scene points, meaning blatant attempts to gain status within a community. Both views are important for a balanced portrayal of BME as a countercultural community, with its own complexities and contradictions.

My analysis of BME's countercultural tactics related to boundaries and membership draws on textual analysis of BME and IAM (BME's community and social network) documents and interviews with site members conducted between 2011 and 2015. These sources are complemented by my own experiences as a member of IAM for over a decade. For a detailed description of the interview process and an extended discussion of reflexivity as it relates to studying a community of which I am a part, see the appendix.

To tell the story of BME and to talk about technological alterity using BME as a field study, I look at sociotechnical factors by identifying and explaining key site features, protocols, and rules; the ways that these factors have changed over time; the ways that they account for community norms of talking about and using the site; and BME's place in a wider context of competing platforms and networks. In the first half of this chapter, I concentrate on BME's rules and norms for participation to establish how this particular countercultural community developed protocols of membership. I focus on the terms of service (TOS) as an example of formalized boundaries of participation, tracing how BME's stated values play out in the removal of site members. The chapter's second half examines BME's struggle to maintain a sense of alterity amid of the increasing popularity of body modification and the rise of social media platforms. In both sections, I highlight the features of technological alterity addressed in chapter 2—legibility, flexibility, and authenticity—as they are expressed in the practices and norms of the BME community.

Context: Key Features of BME and IAM

In referring to BME as a community, I am describing one segment of a group of people who have altered their bodies in some way. Body modification has become widely popular in a short period of time. As of 2014 in the United States, an estimated 25 percent of men and 50 percent of women between the ages of eighteen and thirty-five had tattoos (Blanton 2014). Body modification is an increasingly common practice of self-expression, but for some, it is also a community,[2] and for the last twenty years, BME has positioned itself as an essential online resource for this relationship to modification. BME represents a community of alterity partly because despite the mainstreaming of some forms of body modification, there are still many places where tattoos, piercings, and heavier modifications are still stigmatized: after all, the word *stigma* comes from the Greek *stizein* meaning "to tattoo" (Merriam-Webster 2014). BME is a self-selected group within the modified population. Because body modification plays an important role in their social lives, its members tend to be interested in unusual forms of modifications. Most of the people I interviewed in this community have extensive modifications, including scarifications, silicone or magnetic implants, split tongues, and pointed ears. The people I interviewed described social consequences for having heavier modifications, which they experienced as rejection from mainstream society, whether being the object of unwelcome or hostile attention, being denied entry into places of business, or being discriminated against by employers.

My interest in BME stems from its convergence of alterity, technology, and community, but I do not want to overstate its representativeness of body modification generally. Some of the people I interviewed referred to the need to remind themselves that as diverse and rich as BME felt to them, it did not include all modified folk. For example, Rhoda observed: "It was sort of funny for me to realize that there could be people who are heavily tattooed and heavily modified who are not on BME, who have never heard of BME, who don't want to be on BME. … I think it's important to some people to say that they are part of the IAM or BME community, but it's not the only one." There are also other important online resources related to body modification, including sites like Needled (which became defunct in 2012), Suicide Girls (a blogging and softcore porn site for tattooed and pierced women), and FetLife, a site dedicated to bondage, discipline, dominance and submission, and sadomasochism (generally gathered under the abbreviation BDSM), and fetish culture, which has significant crossover with body modification.

In her early description of digital libraries, Marija Dalbello (2004) compares digital libraries to nineteenth-century cabinets of curiosities. This is also an apt metaphor for the experience of first encountering BME. Rhoda joined IAM in high school, and although her enthusiasm for the site had waned by the time I interviewed her in 2011 (when she was twenty-five), she still recalled the initial sense of shock in her first explorations of BME's content:

> When I went on BME for the first time, it was sort of—the images that you see, a lot of the stuff I wasn't exposed to before, and a lot of it is very heavy. … A lot of people have their own pictures of getting whatever very heavy procedure done, and that just kind of—it didn't freak me out, but I didn't know what to do and how to process what I was seeing.

Rhoda refers here to one of the most commonly used feature of BME—its galleries of photos, videos, and firsthand accounts of modifications (called experiences), which are open to the public, at least to a point. After viewing a set number of galleries, access is no longer free and site membership is required. Special membership is required to view content related to heavier procedures, divided into erotic ("hard") and nonerotic ("extreme") categories of (mostly) heavy genital modification.

The volume of BME's content is enormous (for example, 15,000 photos of tongue piercings and 6,600 narratives on tattoos), but just as difficult to grasp, at least at first, is the range of practices that are gathered under the single label "body modification." Paige was twenty-two at the time of our first interview in 2011 and a newcomer to the site. Like Rhoda, Paige described a process of coming to terms with the many forms of modification depicted on BME:

> Scarification used to shock me. What are people *doing*? Some of the hard stuff—like, I saw a whole bunch of beads on a man's penis. I didn't even know what to think about it. I was so shocked. I was an open-minded person, so I didn't think, "Oh, freaks! It's wrong, gross!" I was just, like, "I don't get it." Now knowing more about suspension and some of the harder activities and stuff like that—I don't understand all of it, but I recognize that people like to push their limits or try new things. I forget how desensitized I am until I'm showing my friends something and they see scarification, and they're like, "Oh, God!" and I go, "Oh, oh, yeah. I remember that freaking me out."

BME's galleries are an important resource for learning about modifications and represent a diversity of modifications, as Rhoda's and Paige's comments indicate. Other public features included a practitioner question and answer section, an international directory of practitioners and shops, a calendar of community events, and a crowd-sourced wiki on procedures, definitions, and key figures in the community. In 2005, BME launched a blog, ModBlog, for registered members and later opened the blog to the public. ModBlog posts interviews with practitioners, discussions of body modification in the news, and photos of modified bodies. An online storefront, BMEshop, which went on indefinite hiatus in 2013, offered body jewelry, BME apparel, piercing supplies, fetish gear, and reference material.

And finally, BME includes a social network site, IAM, which allows users to post individual blog entries, upload photos, and create topic forums. At its peak, IAM had 16,000 members from six continents, predominantly from North America. According to BME's current owner, Rachel Larratt, the site originally was coded to accommodate no more than 19,999 users, and many of the boundary mechanisms that are described later in this chapter were intended to ensure that membership stayed within this upper limit. Of BME's many facets, I concentrate on IAM because it is most closely connected to community dynamics, which provides a useful vantage point for unpacking questions of membership and participation. As Paige noted in her account of deciding to join, "IAM was the next level of getting involved in the community. Submitting stories and stuff is one thing, but when you can go to someone's profile and read about them and send them a message and comment on their forum or something, that's, like, the next level of being involved in the community and getting to know people." In many ways, IAM resembles other social network sites in terms of profile construction. A default IAM page asks users to list their physical location, provide a brief biography, and upload photos. Members can click on links to experiences and photos in the BME galleries and can create galleries of photos (similar to Facebook photo albums) of modifications (such as a gallery that shows photos of receiving and healing a scarification). As in early versions of Myspace (originally MySpace), IAM users are encouraged to tinker with their profiles by choosing images for their page backgrounds and organizing the structure of the page (placement of elements like blog posts and photo galleries). Users can control what number of posts they make per page, whether to allow comments, and whether to display connections to other IAM users. In the remainder of this chapter, I use the acronym *IAM* when talking about the social network site and *BME* to refer to the larger group of features (like the gallery, wiki, blog, and online shop).

IAM users can chat individually through an instant message function. For group conversations, users are encouraged to create and contribute to forums, which are similar to message boards and discuss topics ranging from modified topics (such as jewelry exchange or "Big Lobed Bitches") to more idiosyncratic topics (in a forum called "CTRL V," people post the last thing that they have pasted, and the thread reads like a William S. Burroughs poem or a spam bot). The ability of IAM users to alter the format, design, and privacy settings of their pages exemplifies flexibility as a design ethic. This flexibility is partly an artifact of when IAM emerged. In the late

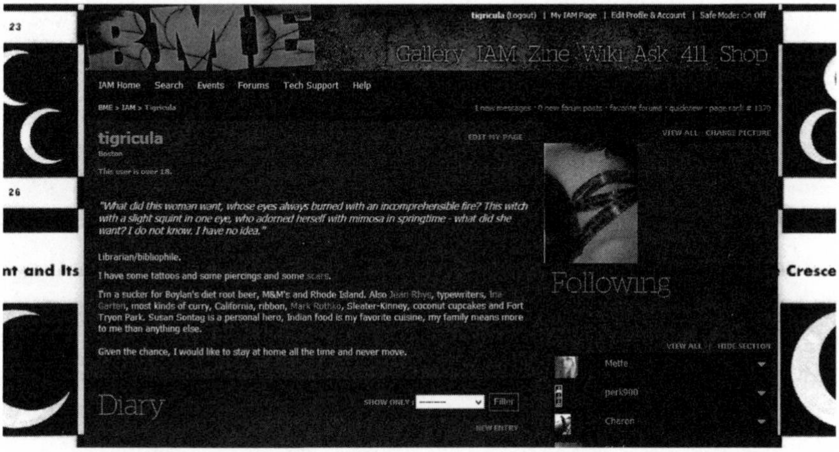

Figure 3.1

A 2014 screenshot of my IAM page. The fundamental design components of the IAM website have remained stable at least since the 1999 version (of which I have not been able to find a screen capture). The current URL for IAM can be accessed through https://www.bme.com/subscribe.

1990s, Internet users were expected to learn at least some hypertext markup language (html) to have an online presence. Rather than plug-ins that automatically insert links to web pages, photos, or other people's profiles, users had to write their own html, at once a burden of technological literacy and an affordance of agency and flexibility. The malleability of IAM also reflects a deeper ethos of individual self-expression. In the context of Myspace, Robert Gehl (2014) and danah boyd (2006) have argued that the mutability of user pages can give a social media platform an overall aesthetic impression of messiness and danger. In IAM's case, the incoherence of user choice amplifies one of BME's banner slogans: "I never wanted to be different. I just wanted to be me."

Context: Transitions in Design and Leadership

In August 2011, BME launched its first major web site redesign in over a decade. The revisions had been in the works for several years. Unlike the 1990s design change from a bulletin board service (BBS) to a "walled garden" site, the new 2011 look was managed by a professional web design company. The redesign was fraught for many reasons, including

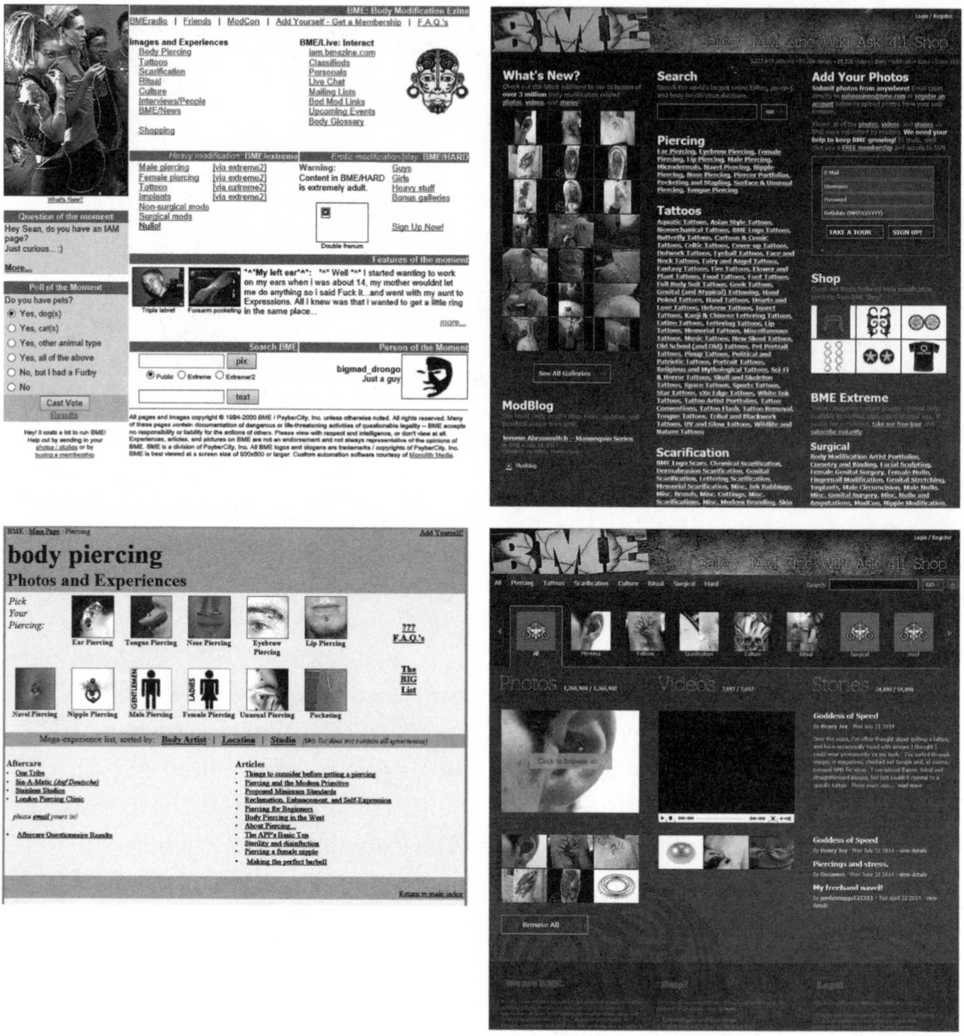

Figure 3.2

Screen captures of BME's main page and galleries in 2000 and 2014.

ballooning costs, difficulties with the design company, and timing (the redesign took place after the 2008 transition of the site's day-to-day operations from the founder, Shannon Larratt, to his former wife, Rachel Larratt). If Mark Zuckerberg has been mythologized as a social media wunderkind, Shannon Larratt is his heavily modified, countercultural alter ego. Shannon attracted a devoted following among body modification enthusiasts and tech geeks, partly because of his commitment to personal self-expression and partly because of his prescience in pioneering tools that became almost default elements of online interactions. In a 2014 interview with Eddie, who was a high school student when he joined IAM in the late 1990s, he described Shannon as a reluctant hero of the modified community: "It's too simple to say that he was a cult leader, but even if he didn't think of himself as one, he was treated as one by a lot of people." After struggling with chronic pain and depression for several years, Shannon committed suicide in 2013. In contrast to the general support for Shannon as a community leader and visionary, many people I interviewed were deeply critical of Rachel, typically characterizing her as a sell-out with only a superficial interest in body modification, despite her longstanding participation in the community and extensive tattoos. Rachel has been largely absent from the site in recent years. She still has an IAM page but has not updated it regularly since 2013. A few users continue to contribute content to IAM and update their pages, yet IAM is currently operating without a clear leadership structure.

I interviewed Rachel Larratt in 2015 after conducting my interviews with site members. With her permission, Rachel is the only study participant who is not given a pseudonym in this book, in keeping with standard research practices regarding people who play a singular role in an institution or a community. Although Shannon and Rachel are critical to BME's evolution as a web site and community, I have downplayed their personal roles in this account because doing so allows me to focus on community standards and norms rather than individual narratives and personalities. I concentrate on documents that relate to BME's and IAM's boundary politics as an online counterculture and interviews that I conducted with site members. Somewhat coincidentally, the first round of interviews was conducted in summer 2011, immediately preceding the relaunch. These interviews offer firsthand accounts of how IAM functioned prior to the redesign (a noticeable decline in activity occurred after 2011). In follow-up interviews and conversations that took place in forums dedicated to the redesign, IAM members discussed the website relaunch as turning away from its earlier design values of legibility as it emulated the professional appearance of mainstream sites and attempted to distance itself from the ethos of censorship and commerciality on display at those sites.

BME's Media Predecessors

With this basic introduction to BME and IAM as a platform, the next section examines the politics of community membership and participation, looking at formal documentations of boundaries and the practices surrounding their enforcement. Before moving on to these topics, however, I briefly address how body modification enthusiasts circulated media and information before the emergence of web-based technologies. BME was not created in a vacuum but rather grew out of existing networks of people technologies and media. As such, what was BME replacing as a sociotechnical assemblage for people with shared interests in and commitments to body modification?

According to Sean, a longtime IAM member and body modification enthusiast, physical mail was a vital communication tool prior to (and even after) the rise of the global Internet. Networks of people who were interested in heavy modifications (particularly genital modifications) connected via a mailing list of names and addresses that was controlled by a single person, who maintained and distributed the physical list for a fee. People typically used the list to trade letters and photos of their modifications. According to a 2014 email from Sean, such lists were the

> go-to source for Modification fans to meet.[3] I think it was $79 for six months—typed out and printed/stapled together, new ads on the last page. Primarily homo and solo sexual, but as time went on more diversity started to show up with straight males, bi males and females joining up, though as I mentioned the women were usually part of a couple.

Sean also explained that his own participation in early networks of body modification content had a lot to do with having a friend who worked as a photo clerk and agreed to process photos of heavy genital modifications discreetly, which was crucial at a time when photographs had to be developed and printed at retail stores or laboratories rather than stored on a personal phone, computer, or digital camera.

Given these earlier practices for circulating information, sharing media, and forming community, what interventions did BME and IAM offer? First, threats of censorship were reduced, in that content was managed by people within the community rather than strangers. When circulating body modification content meant using analog film, people had to physically hand over a roll of film to a store clerk, meaning that a person outside the community saw the customer's face, had access to information written on the film development order form, and had the ability (and in some cases, the obligation)[4] to browse the processed photos and report obscene content to a supervisor and the police. Contrast this with BME's process, in which users could browse photos without revealing themselves in person. Although participating in IAM requires some authenticating information (date of birth, email address, and credit card information for paying members), this information is submitted online rather than in person and is (ostensibly)[5] kept within the community rather than given to a random and potentially judgmental photo clerk. The ability to control content is a huge advantage for any community, but this is particularly true in cases where that content is highly stigmatized.

The second benefit of an online network was that members gained social connections beyond their immediate geographic location. As discussed in the previous chapter, a key part of the Internet's rhetorical emphasis on its connective power focuses on drawing together historically marginalized, geographically dispersed groups. Although I have critiqued this discourse, much of the excitement surrounding BME stemmed from its being a source of community across different kinds of distance. As Eddie explained in his description of IAM as an online community:

> Despite how it ended up, it did establish a community for people who felt extraordinarily alone and isolated—not even geographically, but people thought that nobody else was doing these things. Just the very idea of that knowledge that you are not unique in a bad way, grappling with these impulses, was extremely helpful and therapeutic for a lot of people.

Eddie alludes to a connectivity that offers both reassurance ("you are not alone") and a network (of friends, practitioners, and mentors). In other words, BME provides a point of contact that can draw together users from vastly different places who share stigmatized interests and identities. In the following sections, I consider the different mechanisms of technical and interpersonal control that emerged as BME sought to deliver the promises of the web to the body modification community and also examine the ways that these mechanisms were complicated by internal politics, shifting perceptions of alterity, and competition for online attention.

Participation Matters: IAM's Boundary Politics

All communities have ways of determining membership and establishing boundaries to separate insiders from outsiders. These boundaries can be enforced explicitly or implicitly through formal rules (such as written applications, tests, and contracts) and informal rules (such as shared norms of speech, dress, and behavior). Many communities use both formal and informal rules of membership. For example, passing the bar exam is a highly formal mechanism for joining the professional community of lawyers, but members of the bar also share expectations of how attorneys should dress, talk, and act—both in the courtroom and beyond. In addition to formal boundaries, rituals of membership can be highly sensationalized (such as gang initiations and fraternity hazing) or subtle. Most people who start a new job will monitor coworkers for indications of how to dress, whether to take breaks together or individually, and whether personal phone calls are acceptable at work. All of these minor anxieties stem from acclimating to a new environment and learning appropriate forms of participation. For communities of alterity, the political dimensions of group membership can be exacerbated when activities are illegal or semilegal, potentially subjecting members to legal risks. In BME's case, the politics of membership are not only about legality[6] but also about participation—that is, an interest in building a community that is committed to nonmainstream ideals of bodily aesthetics.

Historically, IAM members have regularly gathered at annual events like the Association of Professional Piercers conference (an industry and a social gathering held in Las Vegas), BMEFest (a yearly gathering of IAM members), and ScarWars (a scarification convention held for several years in the early 2000s). Local groups have met for barbecues, parties, and suspensions and (based on my own experiences of living in New York while being an active IAM member) run into each other at tattoo and piercing shops. Yet although these physical spaces have been important for IAM's sense of community, the main point of connection has been online interactions. This is in contrast to the following two field studies, which have defined physical spaces to anchor their local communities. Shared physical spaces, rules, and practices, including the terms of service (TOS), are a critical means for members to draw together as a group. Communities with strong offline components also need rules and norms to endure, but as documents, the TOS and TOS forum are important mechanisms for developing a sense of coherence and togetherness in a community whose members socialize primarily online.

Membership Mechanisms: Terms of Service as a Living Document

At its most basic level, IAM membership requires modifications, which members demonstrate by submitting content to the BME galleries. Users can avoid paying for site membership as long as they keep submitting photos or experiences. As Rachel described it, "Since the get-go, [IAM membership] has been paid. But our way of [doing it is] either you pay for a subscription, or you submit images, stories, or videos. Basically, everybody pays, but there's ways to do it without using money." Staying a member of IAM requires regular participation, and a no-lurking rule appears early in the conduct section of the TOS.

In addition to renewing membership (by payment or content), site users are required to adhere to standards of conduct that are intended to draw boundaries around IAM as a community. As Mary Douglas (1991) and Sara Ahmed (2000) argue, thinking about boundaries between groups of people is a key mechanism for understanding the richness and granularity of what it means to belong in a community. The complexity of these decisions comes through in Sean's explanation of what does and does not count in his definition of body modification:

> Insiders and outsiders. There's no way to make it sound not elitist. You get to a point where there's a freak show. And it's not my place to judge whether you want to be part of that freak show or not, only to judge whether or not you can be in my sphere. I don't want people who are self-injurers in my sphere. Whereas somebody who has a conscious scarification, I do. So what's the difference? The skin has still been cut. A scar is, has been formed. [Shrugs]

Sean is clear about the arbitrariness of his boundaries, meaning that the decision to include self-injury in a definition of body modification is ultimately subjective. (BME's policy was that self-injury should be included on the site, partly because it was pragmatically infeasible to separate self-injury from experimentation with DIY piercings and tattoos.) As a longtime scene member, Sean's stance is authoritative and informed but not uncontested. Although individual members had their own views on what constituted legitimate versus illegitimate forms of body modification, the most coherent and binding definitions of modification and membership were documented on IAM's TOS.

IAM's TOS: Conceptualizing Countercultural Participation

As a community, IAM experimented with different approaches to allowing (and denying) access to the site. These procedural developments act as guideposts that mark subtle shifts in tactics of boundary control. My analysis relies on the documentation that exists within the site itself and is supplemented with interview material. First, I track changes in IAM's TOS, which informs users about the group's expectations for conduct on the site. I used the Internet Archive's Wayback Machine, a publicly available web service that has regularly cached URLs across the Internet since 1996. By gathering all of the available snapshots of IAM's TOS page, I developed a collection of texts for analyzing IAM's changing rules for membership and user behavior over ten years. As a document, IAM's TOS developed before widely accepted norms of online interactions had been established. As platforms like Facebook, Twitter, and Instagram became dominant players in the social media landscape, their policies and guidelines for user behavior became increasingly similar, to the point that many smaller platforms often copied from bigger sites' TOS and community standards documents (Gillespie, personal communication). In contrast, IAM's TOS grew out of a much more heterogeneous online terrain, with highly idiosyncratic rules for content and behavior. A close reading of the TOS is useful for thinking about what community has meant for IAM members, how it has been operationalized within IAM as a community, and how community guidelines developed in an early moment of Internet history.

When I asked Rachel about the role that IAM's TOS played for the group, she described its purpose as explaining how to treat IAM like a community: "This is our home. We are inviting you into it, but we expect you to behave with certain manners." By thinking of the TOS as a living document and looking at what drops out and what emerges over time, we can detect shifts in what does and does not constitute good behavior.

Second, I look at IAM's TOS violation forum, where administrators logged the removal of users from the site, including the user's alias and specific TOS violation. In some ways, these two artifacts are opposite sides of the same, boundary-maintaining coin. Taken together they articulate the rules on the one hand and the consequences of enforcing those rules on the other.

My analysis here is somewhat technical and document-based because I want to identify in a concrete way the technological and design interventions that IAM administrators devised around questions of membership. What rules and practices emerge for keeping order within a community and for establishing and adhering to community values? What happens (in terms of someone's profile and user status) when these rules are violated? This line of questioning is useful for a broader understanding of how a countercultural community conceptualized participation. This analysis also suggests how norms of participation began to buckle in the wake of new social media platforms that sought a broad rather than narrow user base and a general rather than focused archive of content.

Using the Wayback Machine, I gathered the available snapshots of IAM's TOS page and compared different versions of this document over time, looking at what was added, what dropped out, and what remained the same.[7] Predictably, the TOS expands in each instantiation, growing from 677 words in 2001 to 2,711 words in in 2011 (its most recent version,[8] which is available on the BME wiki). This most recent version claims that the TOS has not been updated since 2002, although this is not completely accurate. For example, references to Shannon Larratt are changed to Rachel Larratt, reflecting the 2008 shift in ownership. The most substantive changes, at least in the snapshots available, took place in 2001 and 2002, and most of my analysis concentrates primarily on this period of stabilization.

One of the biggest changes to IAM's TOS came in the second half of 2001, when the previously unordered list of rules was grouped into seven categories—general philosophy, civility, cost, identity, legal issues, privacy (previously only a subcategory), and miscellaneous. Around the same time, the TOS began to offer more detailed instructions on how to behave. The largest amount of new content was gathered under legal issues and sought to prevent copyright issues as well as spam. For example, the TOS warns against the following:

You agree not to use your site to host free porn.
You may not use your site as a portal to warez/mp3s/passwordz sites.

By late 2001, the civility section emerges, which suggests that a range of new behaviors had surfaced on the site and needed to be addressed. These include hostile messaging, hate speech, and spamming and hacking (such as posting information about events in inappropriate forums or needlessly editing pages so that a user's account would continually show up at the top of IAM's recently updated feed). The TOS reflects back an image of user behaviors that were sufficiently obnoxious to merit being addressed in new TOS language.

In 2002, a statement of community values and politics was added: "The management of this site is very pro-gay, pro-BDSM, pro-alternative politics, pro-civil liberties, etc., and the site's policies are determined in part by these politics and philosophies. If you have particularly conservative views, you may find yourself uncomfortable here." This ideology was present from the start in BME's countercultural content and refusal to tolerate hate speech, but the explicit warning about "conservative views" (where the term *conservative* points both to political and social ideology) is new. The revised language articulates an ideal online public and establishes ideological boundaries around the kinds of discourse and conversation that were expected within IAM.

In addition to the new rules that users were encouraged to follow, there were also new roles they were encouraged to play. In 2002, a shift toward individual user responsibility appears in the form of a "How can you help?" sidebar. The sidebar solicits participation in enforcing the TOS, encouraging users to monitor each other's behavior through a policy of steady escalation. The first request for user help in monitoring behavior suggests that people send offending users a "POLITE message letting them know they're in violation" with a direct link to the TOS. These instructions address "minor" violations. "Serious" violations should be reported, either by emailing an administrator or (for a period between 2005 and 2007) filling out a report form. In the same sidebar, IAM is described as a "dictatorship" because decisions about membership ultimately rest with site administrators. Yet this declaration is immediately followed by a solicitation for comments: "we do appreciate feedback on these rules and IAM in general and are open to change if the community feels it is appropriate."

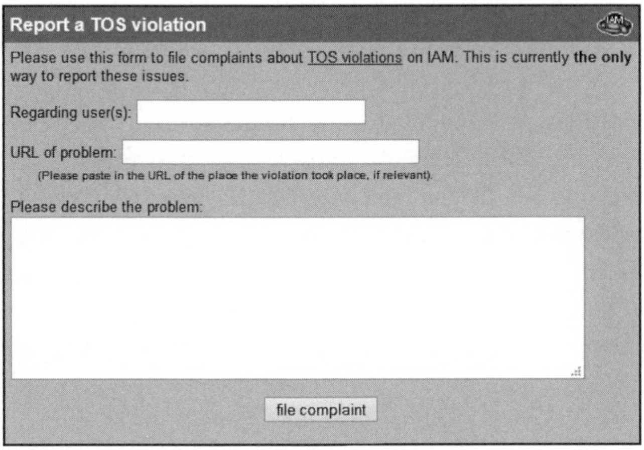
Report a TOS violation

Please use this form to file complaints about TOS violations on IAM. This is currently **the only** way to report these issues.

Regarding user(s):

URL of problem:

(Please paste in the URL of the place the violation took place, if relevant).

Please describe the problem:

file complaint

Figure 3.3
From a February 6, 2006, screen grab, which introduced a simple form for reporting IAM's terms of service (TOS) violations. The TOS form reflected IAM's commitment to a collective enforcement of boundaries and a limited staff for tackling these issues. It offered a technical approach to the social problem of defining and respecting community boundaries.

As the TOS evolves, different levels of participation and new feedback mechanisms emerge for managing community membership. Rather than a linear progression from chaotic democracy to consolidate control, a series of experimental mechanisms fall into and out of favor. As the document evolves over a decade, there are shifts between a model that pushes monitoring responsibilities to the community at large and a model that claims ultimate authority for a small group of administrators. In these shifting policies, I read a struggle to determine the best method of managing a diverse community, particularly in a moment when norms for online communities were still being established.

A third major change in 2002 is the emergence of language that explains how TOS rules are enforced. These procedures (written in italics) deal with bad behavior and explain which violations are more egregious than others. For example, the December 19, 2002, version of the TOS states, "Accounts are for one person only, except by special permission. *First violation gets a warning, second violation results in the deletion of the account.*" The legibility that takes shape here articulates a clear cause and effect, tying specific user actions to particular responses from the site.

These consequences for bad behavior disappear in the most recent wiki version of the TOS, presumably because they are no longer being enforced with any regularity.

The TOS frequently places value in allowing IAM community members to have a degree of responsibility for monitoring membership and for both producing and policing content. The media on IAM are meant to relate to body modification but not violate copyright or child pornography. Body modification defies a straightforward definition. Does weight loss or gain count? How about involuntary versus voluntary amputation? Although the TOS does not define *body modification,* it describes membership in the IAM body modification community as a set of particular practices as well as affiliated politics, sexualities, and values. Another dimension of membership has to do with respecting boundaries regarding content, which is not to be taken outside IAM and thereby reduce BME's claims of dominance in terms of body modification online content. (This expectation of adhering to rules concerning where to post content became more fraught as other, more mainstream social media sites emerged.) IAM membership also meant following norms of reacting to others' content, whether by reporting violations or by avoiding needless interpersonal confrontations. The TOS also identifies practices (such as spam and hate speech) that threaten to undermine IAM's technological and ethical integrity.

A striking feature of reading the TOS permutations over time is the oscillation between informal and formal language. On the one hand, there are idiosyncrasies, as in the instruction "No using IAM to hit on Shannon's girlfriend," which appears (with a hyperlink to Rachel's IAM page) in the June 28, 2001, version and then later disappears. On the other hand, the TOS makes repeated bids for legitimacy with references to legal language and framing. One way of accounting for these fluctuations is to think of IAM as struggling to situate itself between its tactical and strategic interests, to form a community of outsiders while also being self-sustaining. IAM itself is a tactical project, a community-driven staking out of alterity against dominant cultural forms.

As a methodology, closely reading the TOS offers a point of access to how community politics of membership have been operationalized over time. The word *community* often is invoked, left undertheorized, and held up as an unambiguously desirable goal of togetherness or political import, but the many microdecisions that are required to craft social relationships among people who would otherwise be strangers are ignored. Communities may form spontaneously, but they can endure only through a typically messy, iterative process of developing rules and norms. The TOS represents a documentation of this process, and its changes over time point to an effort to make these evolving norms visible and legible.

Having examined the TOS as an evolving document that was intended to be preventative, I turn to a more reactive set of texts—IAM's TOS forum, which documents the suspension and removal of users. The TOS forum is accessible to any IAM member, and (in its current form) spans an eleven-year period, 2003 to 2014 (although the most recent post is from 2011). Dozens of user accounts were removed during that period.[9] Activity on the forum tends to come in spurts. After months or even years of silence, a burst of posts will explain the deletion of a series of accounts, with remarkably consistent explanations of reasons for deleting users' accounts.

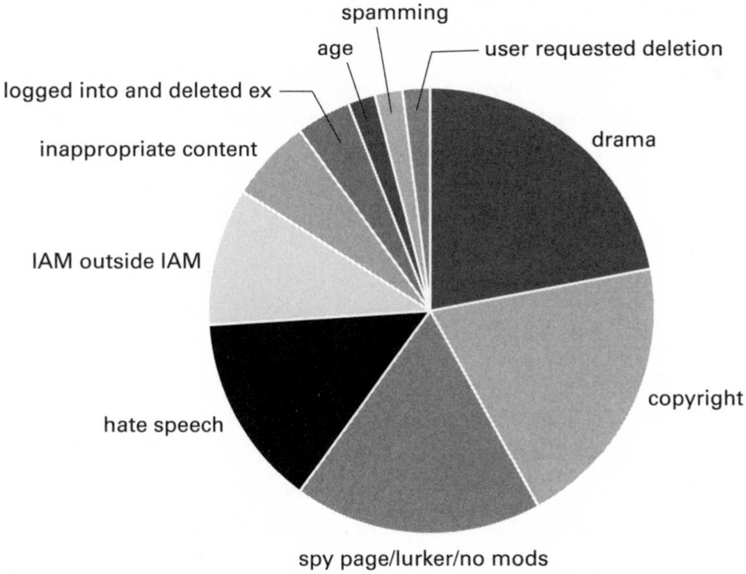

Figure 3.4

An analysis of the violations that were covered in IAM's terms of service (TOS) forum, which includes entries from 2003 to 2011. The data used to create this pie chart came from posts to the TOS forum from an administrator (only four people posted in eight years) and included a user's alias and a brief explanation of the TOS violation. If multiple profiles were linked to the same person, all known user aliases were listed in the description.

The forum contains numerous references to the TOS, and administrators often quote the passages that are relevant to their explanations for removal. In fact, moderators called removing members "TOSing" them, rather like "toading" someone in early online games (deleting the account of a user who breached community standards) (see Dibbell 1998). To TOS someone suggests removal through an appeal to a document or category process of codification, and within the forum post, the only evidence that remains of a removed IAM member is a dead link to their page and (usually) a reference to the TOS rule that he or she violated.

Some categories call for further explanation: "IAM outside IAM" means that a user has taken content from IAM and posted it elsewhere, a different violation than copyright, which involves posting content without attribution or permission. "Logged into and deleted ex" refers to using the password of a former boyfriend or girlfriend to delete the person's account. Hate speech might seem to fall under inappropriate content but is regularly referred to as its own violation. From the outset, IAM was described by its administrators as a site that did not tolerate racist, sexist, or homophobic slurs, which was enforced in forum conversations as well as blog posts, where certain words could trigger a warning pulled from the TOS. Because of this emphasis in the TOS, I separated these violations in my categorizations. Inappropriate content refers to child pornography. Even by the liberal standards of BME, where a video of a woman removing the tip of her own finger is acceptable, depicting minors in porn is considered both legally and ethically objectionable.

The least transparent category, drama, is also the most common. In their work on teens' use of social media, Alice E. Marwick and danah boyd (2014) found that young adult Facebook users deployed the word *drama* to avoid taking sides on an issue. The word *bullying* is never used in the TOS forum, although it is prevalent in mainstream discourses of online harassment. This disparity aligns with boyd and Marwick's (2011) arguments that the word *bullying* is imposed from outside a community and assigns blame to people for acting poorly and inappropriately. The word *drama* may seem self-explanatory, and yet it is not defined explicityly in the forum.

On the one hand, the forum seems to offer a great deal of transparency by pointing interested IAM members to specific violations of an agreement that is fundamental to the site's operation. This is a much more transparent and legible process than is currently typical of platforms like

Facebook or Twitter, where users can flag content as being in some way objectionable but typically cannot follow up on their reports or engage in dialogue with other users on issues of community transgressions (see Crawford and Gillespie 2014). And yet the TOS forum is more of a documentary than participatory process. Despite the sustained push toward inclusivity as the TOS evolved, this inclusion operated more in terms of documentation than adjudication, and some users were almost certainly removed or suspended from the site without being listed in the forum. When asked about the TOS forum, Eddie conjectured that it was largely "performative"—a way to assure users that the TOS was indeed a governing authority over user behavior. The prevalence of the somewhat amorphous label of *drama* supports Eddie's assessment because it allows administrators to display mechanisms of legibility while still allowing less formal, more personal assessments of fit within the community. As a whole, IAM's formal mechanisms for defining and maintaining a division between insiders and outsiders offered some forms of flexibility and legibility by shifting in response to individual user behavior and documenting the operationalization of these boundaries.

External Pressures: IAM under Attack

So far, this discussion of community politics and IAM boundaries has focused on sociotechnical means for managing the threats to community stability that arose from within. In the second half of this chapter, I consider the threats to community integrity that arose from outside forces. As modifications became more popular, the body modification community began to interrogate its own relationship to alterity. In addition, as mainstream social media sites gained popularity, IAM was forced to compete with other platforms for attention and participation. Determining which of these two phenomena happened first or was more consequential is to me less important than considering how both issues problematized the community's existing tactics of producing and circulating content.

With growing access to information and reduced ostracizing of body modification, the tensions that arose from policing online behavior grew more urgent and increasingly contested. Although some community members wanted BME to serve as a resource for anyone with modifications, others wanted to control access to information and media. This struggle is not unique to body modification. As Laura Portwood-Stacer (2013, 61) notes in her analysis of lifestyle politics among anarchist groups, "there is a strategically significant trade-off ... between defending a movement against the diffusion of style for the purposes of maintaining subcultural unity on the one hand and broadening a movement's appeal and increasing the diversity of its participants on the other." IAM's inability to cope with this tension—along with other factors, like widespread dissatisfaction with the site's redesign—contributed to a steady decrease of site use. Instead of dozens of users posting each day, by September 2014, fewer than fifty IAM members had updated their page in the previous month. The main forum, which can be traced back to a 1994 BBS, went without a single post between September 2014 and July 2015. To understand this decline, I examine the ways that BME responded to mainstream media representations of body modification and the kinds of pressures that surfaced as other social media platforms disrupted established norms of online counterculture.

Outside In: Modification Goes Mainstream

Many of the boundary practices that are described in the prior section refer to the violation of IAM's rules by individual members. Yet perhaps the biggest threat to BME's stability as a community was external rather than internal—namely, the increasingly common depictions of body modification in the mainstream media, which undermined BME's dominance in documenting its own alterity. Arguably, BME's most valuable resource was the content provided by its users about their modifications, and that content needed to be controlled to retain its value. This view resonates with Sarah Thornton's (2013, 90) comment that the British club music scene "sees itself as an outlaw culture, but its main antagonist is not the police (who arrest and imprison) but the media, who continually threaten to *release* its cultural knowledge to other social groups." Television shows like *Inked* and *Miami Ink* (both of which launched in 2005) represented the release of countercultural content far beyond the confines of the body modification community. With the rise in media attention, community boundaries became increasingly destabilized, opening up divides along access and belonging. This is not to say that the community had formerly existed in a state of uncontested agreement about insiders and outsiders, which should be clear from the review of IAM's terms of service forum above. But the emergence of mainstream depictions of body modification represented a fundamental shift in terms of where information about these practices could be found and how it was narrated, disrupting BME's monopoly of access.

Many of the people that I interviewed were harshly negative of mainstream media portrayals of body modification, particularly TV shows. Mr. Pink, a piercer in Tennessee, was twenty-eight years old when I spoke with him in 2011. His antagonism toward shows that purported to document his career was representative of people that I interviewed: "I feel like a lot of these TV shows—granted, they expose a lot more people to what we do, but they really cheapen it as well." There is a delicate tipping point here between visibility that allows for reducing stigma and exposure that commercializes and misappropriates, imposing new narratives on longstanding practices.

Sean was also critical of the "confessional" trope of tattoo-based reality shows, where clients are asked to explain the meanings behind their tattoos. Conventionally, this dialogue takes place at the behest of a tattoo artist as clients are being tattooed and are often visibly emotional. Margo DeMello (2000, 151–158) argues that the development of personal narratives for tattoos was critical to the middle-class appropriation of tattooing from its working-class roots, representing a class-based mainstreaming of body modification. Beyond simply not liking the mass-market portrayal of tattoos, Sean dismissed the idea that modifications require some sort of explanatory logic: "Don't think that we're a commodity, just because of *Miami Ink*, because of seeing piercing in a newspaper. It's OK to not understand why we do this stuff. *Miami Ink* has taught us that everything has to have a story, and it doesn't. [My girlfriend] has big pretty jewelry in her ears *because* she has big pretty jewelry in her ears. I have tattoos on my fingers *because* I have tattoos on my fingers." Sean resists (and resents) the emergence of new cultural forms that come to dictate expectations of how body modification is evaluated and discussed. Although conversations about motivations for procedures sometimes took place within the modified community, mainstream media portrayals of modification led to a presumption that those conversations were presumed not just highly emotional but necessary.

Sean and Mr. Pink object to the commercialization of body modification and what they consider to be the "cheapening" of the community through the linking of modified bodies with "commodities." The sense that mainstream media reduces alterity to a set of explanatory tropes is part of what provoked struggles over membership within the community. Portwood-Stacer (2013, 23) has noted of anarchist communities that "subcultural commitments to 'authenticity' are both productive—in that they engender self-discipline and community accountability among activists—and destructive—in that they often lead to internecine drama and boundary policing within movements." In the case of BME, many of these tensions of ownership of online content related to body modification came to a head with the 2011 relaunch of IAM.

When I interviewed Rachel Larratt in 2015, she explained the decision to hire a company to redesign the site rather than have staff members do the design work in-house (as IAM had done previously) because the IAM staff was too overworked to find the time to upgrade badly outdated code. After she hired a design company, the question became how to manage tensions between longtime community members who were nervous about change and people who increasingly expected features that were available on mainstream sites like Facebook. As Rachel described it during our interview,

> What I originally wanted to do was pick the exact same [interface] but just redesigning the back end so that people won't even know. But I got so much criticism from the programmers involved and other people—like, "We can't keep up with everybody else, and now we're just going to fall further and further behind." Stuff like that.

The fear of falling behind mainstream sites motivated IAM's redesign, but it set up a conflict with the expectations of long-term users who were accustomed to a simple interface that dated back to the late 1990s.

The redesign presented a crucial juncture for the IAM community. When I conducted interviews in 2011, participants were cautiously optimistic about the promised improvements and curious to see upgraded features. But when the upgrade was launched after a series of delays, the response was almost entirely negative. The site was buggy, but IAM lacked a dedicated support staff to assist users quickly and consistently. People began deactivating or deleting their accounts, and participation dropped among those who stayed. When I conducted follow-up interviews in 2014, participants referred to the redesign as deeply flawed and tended to assign blame to Rachel rather than Shannon, even though the code upgrade had been planned long before his departure from the site.

After the site was relaunched, administrators set up an ideological dynamic in which sites like Facebook were positioned as corporate and commercial and BME's site was cast as both countercultural and a site of belonging. For example, a forum was set up on IAM so that users could ask questions about the upcoming redesign. In May 2012, ten months after the relaunch, Rachel Larratt posted to the forum:

> Things are changing. We're trying to make everything work but things like Facebook make it impossible to have the same active community that we had before FB blew up. If you think back to it, there was nothing but BME/IAM for almost a decade. I can't compete with a company that has a billion dollars in "value," 700 full time programmers, hundreds of millions of members and every single commercial on TV promoting them but I'm not trying to compete. I'm trying to continue to make a home on the internet where people who are like minded can hang out and feel safe. To me, other sites feel like going to the mall or being out in a gigantic parking garage. I want IAM to be the home that it always has been. Help me figure out how to do that.

Part of the allure of IAM was that it was a space where people could connect and offer mutual resources of information about body modification, which many IAM members describe as a kind of "journey." Even for people who have less teleological understanding of body modification, this sense of a shared interest largely defines IAM as a community. As Randy stated in a 2011 interview, "I'd call IAM a community because people share a common interest. You can't say that about Facebook." IAM had persisted in the face of other social media sites, but Facebook represented a new kind of competition—a strategic force in contrast to other more tactical sites, like Makeout Club and tribe.net.

Beyond the characterization of Facebook as a generic "mall" of social media, other ideological differences emerged between these platforms in terms of boundaries and participation. One pivotal anecdote comes from Shannon Larratt's explanation of why he returned to *ModBlog* as a contributing writer in 2012, four years after Rachel Larratt took over as solo owner of BME. It would be difficult to overstate how surprising many people found his return, given the degree of interpersonal tensions surrounding the 2008 change in BME ownership. Shannon explained his decision as the result of frustrations that other platforms—specifically, Facebook—offered inadequate means of ensuring free speech. After two instances of having his body modification content flagged as inappropriate, Shannon was locked out of his Facebook page, prompting the following response in a *ModBlog* post (Larratt 2012):

> Now, I don't believe Facebook specifically has it in for me, or for body modification. I think they simply couldn't care less about us one way or the other, leaving us at the mercy of automated systems that boot us off or slap us with petty punishments the second some[one] complains. I have been speaking out against rebloggers who simply repost pictures they steal from BME as their own, and I have been speaking out against tattoo blogs that objectify women needlessly—for all I know one of them is laughing all the way to the bank, having found an easy way to manipulate the system. Well, they've managed to push to somewhere that they can't censor me. For now, I'm taking my writing to hear [sic] on ModBlog. Tattoo artists and piercers beware—all it takes is your competition making a few mouse clicks, and you'll go through the same hell. Make sure you have a backup plan like BME, because, to again state the obvious, **Facebook is not your friend**.

Shannon provides a rich set of claims about online censorship and alterity, presenting harsh criticisms of reposting content without attribution, objectifying and sexualizing women's bodies, and commercializing alterity, viewpoints that echo the values expressed on IAM's TOS. His anger targets the illegibility of Facebook's censorship process and the intractable and arbitrary mechanisms of flagging content, themes that surface again in chapter 5's discussion of drag and queer identity on Facebook. Shannon's assessment underscores my arguments about the importance of legibility as a value of digital technology within this particular countercultural community. But Shannon's positioning of BME as a "backup plan" for self-expression is a problematic content model for a community that required continuous and committed participation from its members.

In their analysis of social media flagging as a system of crowd-sourced behavior and content regulation, Kate Crawford and Tarleton Gillespie (2014, 413) noted that flags are subject to imprecision, opacity, and misuse and that as tools of adjudicating behavior and content, flags "leave little room for the articulation of concern, and that articulation is bound up within an individual message to the platform, resulting in an opaque decision by the platform." In contrasting IAM's approach to TOS violations with the policies that Shannon lambasts, IAM's process for removal emerges as far more transparent and more clearly connected to an expressed set of (countercultural) values than Facebook's process was. Crawford and

Gillespie suggest that a lack of transparency and granularity in flagging systems can lead to a misuse of flags because of animosity or prejudice. Shannon's *ModBlog* post offers examples of potential misuses, including the use of flags to harass others or to discriminate against heavily modified people, who might be perceived as freaks.

Facebook constituted a threat not only because its immense popularity represented competition for user attention but also because its values were amorphous. This lack of political values could have been construed as an opening for IAM to make itself more necessary, and yet to the extent that this attempt was ever made, it was ultimately inadequate as a lure, as Eddie pointed out in a 2014 interview:

> There was an opportunity [for IAM] to say, "You're not going to get banned here for graphic images or whatever, like you would on Facebook or anything else. Ultimately, it seemed like people didn't care—like that was not enough of a selling point. They said, "Well, we could find other ways. We have all sorts of ways to share these photos."

Between Shannon's outrage and Eddie's explanation is a wager of values, where BME and Facebook could coexist only as long as users saw value in both, which also required seeing them as distinct. After the redesign and as (some forms of) body modification began to be mainstreamed, however, the distinction between the two platforms became increasingly blurred.

Inside Out: Holding the Line within the Community

In a way, the growing popularity of mainstream social media platforms tested members' commitments to BME as a countercultural community. From the administrator's perspective, BME's reputation rested on being the most authoritative, accurate, and reliable site for gathering content related to modifications. As members began posting content in other platforms, BME's monopoly on information threatened to unravel. Before the rise of social network sites, the exchange of media related to countercultural practices like body modification often involved a level of secrecy, as reflected in the tightly controlled mailing lists that predated online circulations of content. In contrast, a powerful share-everything ethic surrounds most social media platforms (Marwick and boyd 2011). IAM members were familiar with the share-everything pull of social media after years of being encouraged to contribute content to BME's galleries, pages, and forums. But when it became possible to share on less exclusive platforms like Myspace and Facebook, IAM's administrators became increasingly concerned. In the redesign forum, administrators repeatedly asked users to keep body modification content on BME rather than mainstream sites or at the minimum not to post such content on a site like Facebook until after they posted it on BME. As an administrator pleaded in May 2010, a full year before the relaunch happened: "And since this is something that most people will be doing anyway, the only thing that BME says is 'Hey, when you upload that stuff to Facebook, upload them here too.'"

Tensions over when and how to share content were magnified when procedures were quasi-legal and risked exposing practitioners to prosecution. In our initial 2011 interview, Sean described the deterioration in the context of events where extreme modifications were taking place:

> I just don't think secrecy is there. … And I think the last bastion of people who tried to keep secrets, aren't really that good at it, myself included. Because of technology, because of Tumblr and the Twitter and the Internets, I find myself at events taking pictures and [then putting them] online when they're happening. And of course, you want to show people the fun stuff you're doing. I've been guilty of it. And if I'm such an ardent critic of it and I'm still doing it, imagine people who aren't a critic of it?

Somewhat ruefully, Sean admitted to violating the norms of content control that he felt were desirable because posting across platforms was simply too attractive to him. Before the emergence of mainstream social media sites, BME members could experience the thrill that Sean mentions of sharing new modifications, but they did so in the context of a community that had formal as well as informal means of responding to modification-related content. Other community members were less circumspect, however, and even welcomed the opening up of body modification practices beyond a confined community. For example, Chris stated that

> It would be better if [extreme body modification] got more acceptable because then it would mean people could have facial tattoos and be working at McDonald's. The more it's out, the more accepted it is, the more that people don't have to worry about tattooing their hands, tattooing their face, and hold down a square job. Because now, there's no way a lawyer could have a facial tattoo and get any kind of reputation or business at all. The more accepted it is, the more mainstream, the better.

Chris's stance is pragmatically focused on the real-world consequences of heavy body modifications for individuals rather than the survival of IAM as an online community.

As new social media platforms arrived, IAM members were drawn to the promise of a wider audience. The contradiction here is between identifying with and wanting to maintain a sense of alterity while at the same time reaffirming one's marginality by displaying countercultural behavior to the mainstream. On IAM, photos of getting a split tongue could signal belonging, but on Facebook, it could potentially go viral globally. Technically, these two need not be in opposition, given that activity on one site does not prohibit activity elsewhere. A user could obtain specific information on how to heal an obscure procedure on IAM, for example, while also posting content to Facebook. And yet there is an economy of attention at stake here, which exposes the limits of thinking of online content as nonrivalrous.

In discussions of online content sharing, participants commonly celebrate the fact that unlike traditional media formats, digital files can be shared with others without giving up the original version. Access to a wide array of content is frequently cited as central to the democratic and liberatory possibilities of the Internet, as is discussed in the previous chapter. But platforms do compete for participation, even if the same content can proliferate across sites at almost no cost. When IAM users were given the choice between posting content for thousands versus billions of users, they first shared in both and then increasingly posted only for the vastly larger audiences on Facebook and Instagram.

Mainstream portrayals of body modification brought another, somewhat disquieting, consequence of competing for status. With increasing commercialization of basic practices like piercing and tattooing, some people within the modified community began to pursue modifications not because of a personal commitment or self-journey but simply because the borders of alterity were being redrawn. As I noted earlier, body modification involves a wide range of practices, and IAM members tended to associate their online community with more extreme forms of modification. The division between common and extreme forms of modification and the related practices of documenting and circulating modifications pushed some people into considering heavier work as a means of gaining status.

The most disturbing narrative I encountered of pushing bodily boundaries for the sake of membership status came from Sean. During a discussion of how increased mainstream attention to body modification had affected BME, Sean described meeting a person who opted to get a subincision (an uncommon genital modification) as a way of securing an invitation to ModCon, a highly exclusive, BME-sponsored gathering of people who are interested in obtaining extreme procedures:

> You had people who didn't know they wanted to do this stuff until they saw it and made really questionable permanent decisions. We're talking about people who decided to get subincisions as scene points. Because, this is a direct quote, "Of all the BME modifications, this seemed like the easiest way to get into ModCon." I need you to let that sink in. Think about having your penis cut from the tip of the urethra organ to your scrotum. You won't urinate the same. You won't ejaculate the same. Your jeans or underwear rubbing in that opening will cause you either immense pleasure or discomfort, and you're doing that because it seems like the easiest way to be accepted by the peers you liked. It's mind blowing.

Obtaining scene points was always a possibility on IAM, as it is with almost any countercultural group (Thornton 2013). But as mainstream media exposed body modification to a wider audience, the struggle to hold on to a sense of alterity became more intense.

Writing about "enhancement technologies," Carl Elliott (2003) describes the struggle between trying to fit in and trying to be unique, between conformity and individuality. These efforts are always problematic because our social worlds are complex. Signals of fitting in for one community can lead to ostracizing in another, and communities tend to condemn attempts to fit in that seem motivated by false (or desperate) pretenses. Sean's claim that "people who didn't know they wanted to do this stuff until they saw it" brings visibility to the forefront of culpability. BME established its own politics of visibility in which exposure to content required participation, and this reciprocity might not have been universally fair but did facilitate the exchange of context and perspective from within the community.

As social media sites became increasingly popular, new modes of making visible and renarrating countercultural practices disrupted prior approaches to managing membership in online communities of alterity. Concerns about visibility, context, and access became more salient (and problematic) as representations of alterity emerged from mainstream media institutions and mainstream social media sites. Between its contentious site redesign and its transition in leadership, IAM began to feel more commercial and less countercultural. Expectations for community participation were still legible but began to wane as BME struggled to carve out a distinct role for itself and its users within a wider ecology of digital cultural production. BME needed to be more than a back-up plan for social media participation, but as the values and services of that enhanced BME remained elusive, the site became less and less necessary as a source of information for people with interests in body modification and eventually was rendered nearly obsolete.

Conclusions

I first joined IAM in 2004 to track down a practitioner, whom I will call Ben, who was currently between shops. Online links pointed me to Ben's IAM page, which was accessible only to other IAM members. When I joined, I intended to leave after learning more about Ben and his next shop. Ten years (and 665 blog posts) later, I still have a user account and still am a client of Ben's. In 2011, I messaged Ben on IAM to schedule an appointment, and he responded, "Hit me up on Facebook. I never use this site anymore." Clearly, the technological landscape had shifted drastically. In 2004, IAM had been essential for connecting me to a particular practitioner when I lacked local knowledge of body modification resources. By 2011, that site was almost useless and eclipsed by Facebook as a communication platform.

While visiting IAM's jewelry exchange forum (where users can sell or trade jewelry), I found a March 2012 conversation between IAM members about a Facebook group that served the same function:

User 1: Probably no point posting judging on how dead iam is nowadays, but I'm after a kaos earskin in 6mm in the shortest length they do, anybody help me out?
User 2: There is a Facebook group now.
User 3: Woah, where is the FB group? Link that shit!
User 1: Seconding the request for a link to the fb group ☺
User 2: [link]
User 1: thankies!

What struck me about this exchange was the lack of investment in maintaining IAM as a site, that users seemed unconflicted and even excited about simply migrating to Facebook.[10] Were the stakes that low? Was Facebook simply interchangeable as an alternative, at least in terms of what mattered most to people who were seeking a body modification community?

In a way, the story of BME is that of a countercultural community that failed—or a countercultural community that could not survive the mainstreaming of modification or the competition of bigger, more technologically sophisticated social media platforms. And yet studying sites like IAM provides a richer, more complex understanding of the Internet and the communities that it hosts. Rhetoric around the popularity of mainstream social media sites like Facebook and Twitter can make it seem as though these platforms sprang up out of nothing, when in fact they developed beside and in competition with niche sites that had their own practices, values, and sociotechnical relationships. As a field study environment, IAM also offers important clues into how countercultural identities and practices fare in platforms that cater largely to the center rather than margins.

One way of evaluating IAM's struggle to retain its membership is to consider the redesign as a battle over IAM's different constituencies and different visions of counterculture. In his analysis of "platform" as a technopolitical metaphor, Tarleton Gillespie (2010, 348) argues that

> The term *platform* helps reveal how YouTube and others stage themselves for these constituencies, allowing them to make a broadly progressive sales pitch while also eliding the tensions inherent in their service: between user-generated and commercially produced content, between cultivating community and serving up advertising, between intervening in the delivery of content and remaining neutral.

The decline of IAM came about in large part because it was unable to satisfy wildly opposite constituencies—its base of countercultural users as well as an undefined (at least publicly) mass of future users. In this light, the 2011 site redesign represented a bid to appease a particular constituency over its existing user base and came to symbolize IAM's inability to satisfy either. It is uncertain whether maintaining IAM as a rudimentary but still functioning site would have been preferable to a redesign that alienated many and satisfied few.

There are no tidy parallels between marginalized groups and their stripped-down design and mainstream groups and their technological sophistication. Instead, the tensions around IAM's redesign can be read as an indication of how a platform's interface can matter deeply to people who use the site on a daily basis and of how localized debates can emerge from decisions that may at first seem purely technical. Arguably, design and interface decisions become even more crucial for groups that rely on online (rather than offline) interactions as the core source of community.

The dynamic between Facebook and BME points to an ideological contest that is larger than two social media sites that battle for users and content. The IAM members that I interviewed concentrated on the site's redesign as a key tension in its decline, but the issue cannot be read as purely a matter of features, functions, or aesthetics. As mainstream social media sites become increasingly popular, they establish norms for how people should treat content, data, and each other. IAM's trial-and-error approach to managing members illustrates how dynamic early online communities were compared to how locked down social media sites tend to be now. Although the designs of social media sites like Facebook are frequently tweaked, administrators make these changes without notifying users or asking for their consent. Many mainstream sites use A/B testing (dividing users into two groups, subjecting each group to a different treatment, and then monitoring any changes in behavior) and do not inform users that the interface and features that they are interacting with are different from those that other users are seeing. The design decisions that unfold as a result of these choices have financial, legal, and social consequences. In chapter 5, I return to this comparison between mainstream and countercultural values in an examination of how sites regard names, identity, users, agency, and legibility.

During follow-up interviews, I asked participants what IAM could have done differently in its design relaunch. Several people suggested an explanation for BME's decline that relates less to design and more to the moment in time that BME emerged. In Eddie's assessment,

> maybe [it] just stopped being quite as important to be naked and covered in blood on the Internet. ... [IAM] was a lot of younger people. As they're getting older, maybe they realized, "I want to have everything in one place. I want a website whose design I understand—that's not run by people whose interpersonal relationships are going to destroy the site that I'm on." You lose something by going to Facebook or Twitter or whatever community ends up housing these people. You do lose the more personal element of it, but you also gain a sense of consistency that I guess is important for communities as well.

Eddie's explanation points to historical context as a way of understanding IAM as a phenomenon. Body modification (in the United States, at least) is most popular in late adolescence and early adulthood, which was also the case for social media use in the late 1990s to early 2000s, when BME was most successful. So one possible reason for BME's decline is that its members aged out of the site. Moreover, these site members could not be replaced by younger people because they were used to platforms like Facebook, Twitter, and Instagram, which had bigger audiences and more sophisticated design features. The commitment to legibility that guided IAM's membership policies and original design were reasonable when social media platforms were new and their politics were in flux. After new norms (including expectations for participation and sophisticated interfaces) took root, IAM's ethics were too dated and too untenable.

Although BME ultimately was unable to cope with the disruptions of mainstream social media and mainstream body modification, the lessons that its experiences can provide are multiple. First, alterity is a double-edged sword. It lures both desired community members who share interests and values and gawkers who have superficial interests that can objectify alterity. Protecting a sense of alterity is vital to maintaining countercultural identity and community, but it also can lead to destabilizing games of one-upmanship, scene points, and commodification. In many ways, online platforms exacerbate issues of alterity and belonging by making these interpersonal rivalries more visible or even gamifying them. Second, a community's commitment to legibility in its design and user policies can be an important means of drawing users together but raises the stakes for site redesign. My analysis of IAM's terms of service points to administrators' attempts to make community membership legible, but BME's survival could have been made more likely by a similar commitment to legibility in leadership and communications to IAM members about transitions of power and control. If communities cannot assert their perspectives and values, in terms of content or membership policies, they might not survive. The simultaneous mainstreaming of body modification and social media destabilized BME's previously unchallenged monopoly on content, and the site ultimately could not retain the members whose participation sustained BME's content and its sense of community.

4 They Came from the Basement: Tactics of Secrecy in New Brunswick's Underground Punk Community

Going to a punk rock show in New Brunswick, New Jersey, is not like going to punk shows in most other places. To attend a basement show, you head to a one- or two-story house on a tree-lined street in a residential neighborhood. Passing a few college-age smokers out front, you find your way to the backyard of the house. At the basement entrance, someone collects money, usually around $5. If you happen to be reluctant to pay the cover charge, whether because the band is unknown or you are short of cash, you are reminded that all money goes to bands to cover food and gas and that payment is an important part of keeping the scene alive. Paying bands even a modest amount encourages other acts to book shows in New Brunswick over other cities in the Philadelphia to New York corridor and to play in a house basement rather than at a bar or a club. Past the door, you move downstairs to join the crowd of other music enthusiasts, steps away from the musicians. The basement walls are probably lined with mattresses or padded envelopes (courtesy of the U.S. Postal Service) for sound insulation and decorated with blinking strands of lights and collages of stickers with band names and logos. Sometimes the crowds are large, and the basement feels cramped and claustrophobic. At other times, performers and audience members are in equal number, which can feel either intimate or awkward. People smoke and drink, ashing cigarettes and dropping bottles onto the floor. Fans, band members, and basement hosts occasionally circulate with zines or flyers for upcoming shows.

If one term sums up the aesthetics and politics of New Brunswick's basement community, it is *do-it-yourself* (DIY), which refers to an ethic of favoring self-sufficiency over commercialized products and services. Students from the nearby university often form local bands, and the scene operates without formal venues or professional bookers. Yet hundreds of bands come through town each year, playing in a dozen or so houses that make up a loose network of informal venues that change from one year to the next. The same DIY ethics that lead New Brunswick punks to host shows in their houses and run their own labels also applies to the norms and politics of how they use technologies, shape the physical spaces of basements as venues, and carry out the everyday practices of communication and information sharing. Methods of using digital technologies in the basement community reflect DIY values and a particular attitude toward communication about shows. New Brunswick punks have developed (and enforced) a rigorous set of controls around sharing information about shows to avoid unwanted attention from the police and other local authorities. These rituals of communication work across a range of digital and nondigital technologies to thwart attempts to shut down shows and solidify a sense of countercultural identity.

As a locus of punk music and practice, New Brunswick's basement community sees itself as countercultural because of its quasi-legality, which relies on DIY organization and employs information tactics of secrecy. The illegality or quasi-legality of shows stems from a number of factors.[1] Show houses are residences, not professional venues, and do not possess licenses to host events that charge money for attendance. At most shows, alcohol flows freely, minimal attempts are made to curtail underage drinking, and people often smoke, even when basements are crowded and soundproofed with highly flammable materials. These conditions risk disapproval from neighbors, landlords, fire marshals, and police, so avoiding official detection of shows has become a critical feature of the community's relationship to digital technologies.

Given these motivations for maintaining control over show information, New Brunswick's basement community provides a valuable opportunity for examining tactical flexibility, information sharing, and online technologies in terms of secrecy. Secrecy is often important to countercultural communities, either because their activities operate in a legal gray area (the case for both New Brunswick basement punks and the practitioners of heavy body modification procedures who are discussed in the previous chapter) or because they prefer that their activities take place without mainstream awareness. The sociotechnical tactics of secrecy in the basement community, supported by both DIY and punk values, defy certain expectations of digitally mediated communication. In a share-everything paradigm of online communication, the basement community presents a share-some-things ethic, supported both by DIY and punk values.

Because New Brunswick's basement community is populated largely by young people, it is a particularly interesting site for studying practices of self-censorship and media reduction. Although a dominant narrative of college students depicts them as being permanently wired, social media dependent, and hyperindividualized, members of the basement scene are committed to the mindful use of both online and offline communication tools in the service of a collective need for keeping secrets. This chapter looks at the various tactics that have developed and endured within the community, both to avoid police detection of shows and to police each other. I concentrate on the range of tactics (both online and offline) that members use to protect the community from law enforcement and maintain its countercultural exclusivity.

Fieldwork for this project, which started when I was a graduate student living in New Brunswick, was deeply collaborative. I first began exploring this field site with my fellow graduate students Aaron Trammell and Nathan Graham and assistant professors Joe Sanchez and Mor Naaman. As a New Jersey native and longtime punk enthusiast, Aaron was our entry point into the community as the work grew into a multifaceted project on information practices and secrecy (Lingel, Trammell, Sanchez, and Naaman 2012). Researching the basement community had three basic parts—participant observation, a focus group with longtime community members, and individual interviews with scene newcomers, band members, and people who hosted shows in their houses. The bulk of this research was conducted collectively between 2009 and 2010, and I revisited the sites independently in 2014 and 2015 for further observation.

After providing some background information on New Brunswick as a geographically and temporally bound locus of punk music, I address concepts of DIY and secrecy, both of which are vital to understanding why this community operates as it does. I describe online and offline tactics for avoiding unwelcome attention to music events and describe two occasions when these tactics were either ignored or set aside, demonstrating the consequences for violating community norms and values. This chapter examines the sociotechnical practices of the New Brunswick basement community to show how digital technologies can be used in the service of secrecy and where these practices fall short. In contrast to the inflexibility and illegibility of dominant social media platforms, sociotechnical networks and assemblages of the punk community are characterized by a high degree of malleability and localized values.

Context: New Brunswick's Geography and DIY Ethics

Although there are fairly consistent, identifiable rules for how basement shows operate, it is more difficult to obtain a clear understanding of how the community began. One participant cited a backyard performance by the 1980s hardcore band Black Flag as integral to the scene's genesis. Another participant pointed to the DIY praxis of the punk band Minutemen (also from the 1980s) as an influential model of values and ethics for building a sustained punk community. Still others argued that the community was fueled by small bands that played shows in New Brunswick as they traveled between New York and Philadelphia.

Without denying the significance and influence of bands like Black Flag and the Minutemen, I find the geographic explanations particularly persuasive. New Brunswick marks a halfway point between the sizable cultural centers of New York and Philadelphia, meaning that large bands tend to skip over it in favor of large venues (and fan bases) and small bands use the city as a stopping point between these large scenes. Home to Rutgers, the state's largest university, New Brunswick counts approximately forty thousand college students among its eighty thousand residents. Unlike many college towns (like Lawrence, Kansas, or Madison, Wisconsin), New Brunswick, New Jersey, has few professional venues for live music, particularly for people who are under age twenty-one. At the time of this writing, only the long-established Court Tavern offered shows for people age eighteen and over, leaving a sizable population of college students in search of local entertainment. The basement community helps mitigate this shortage, and New Brunswick enjoys a reputation as a breeding ground for launching relatively successful indie and punk bands (such as the Bouncing Souls, Gaslight Anthem, and the Screaming Females), where part of the origin stories of these bands draws on the community's commitment to DIY organization. Together, the different components of New Brunswick's geography make it a logical place to host live music for the benefit of a fairly large audience of college-age people. In the absence of official concert locations, private house basements fill the vacuum, relying on a DIY mentality of collective commitments to under-the-radar shows.

Members of the New Brunswick scene are proud of their community and its reputation. As one participant, Jay, observed:

> People in the know, all across the country and even internationally, look at New Brunswick as a destination. Many are the times when they're like, "We just couldn't wait to get to New Brunswick"—those who had been there before. We make a concerted effort through the quality of the shows, through the quality of the party we throw them afterwards when they stay here. We try to send every touring band off to saying: "Wow, New Brunswick rules!"

The community's self-regard, which stems from both the quality of the shows and the ways that they are produced, reenforces members' determination to maintain their social commitments to DIY values and technological tactics of secrecy.

Broadly defined, DIY holds that the act of "producing is as crucial as what is produced" (Rivett 1999, 43), meaning that maintaining community control over how production (of media, information, or tools) takes place is as important as the results of these efforts. Steven Gelber (1997) traces DIY values to postwar home improvement projects, although the main contemporary associations with DIY are with zine (Duncombe 1997), anarchist (Portwood-Stacer 2013), and punk (Waksman 2004) communities. DIY also has connections to maker spaces (Fox, Ulgado, and Rosner 2015) and other forms of media activism, like alternative radio (Dunbar-Hester 2010, 2014; Pursell 1993; Turner 2006; see also a collection on DIY citizenship edited by Ratto and Boler 2014). In all of these projects, learning how to use and build media technologies can enable a group to control its own content and open up access to other communities, dialogues, and resources. Within New Brunswick's basement community, the dominant conceptualizations of DIY are tied to a loosely Marxist critique of capitalist systems of labor, where anticorporate commitments are fundamentally understood as a collective rather than individual project. And yet there is also a way in which the basement community's DIY practices are playful, a form of improvisation and experimentation that reflects collective creativity and skills. DIY values (of self-sufficiency, playful arrangements of technology, and bottom-up organization tactics) are deeply embedded into the community's practices and self-perceptions.

Context: Secrecy/Privacy

Throughout this chapter, I use the words *secrecy* and *privacy*, which have important differences in meaning. Existing research on online technologies have made privacy a focal point, reflecting social and political concerns about maintaining privacy while using online platforms to communicate, document everyday life, complete business transactions, and engage culturally (see Cohen 2012; Livingstone 2008; Nissenbaum 2010). Following Don E. Merten (1999), I use the word *secrecy* to refer to information that is tied to a group. It is distinct from the word *privacy*, which refers to information that is grounded in the personal. In other words, secrecy involves keeping what *we* do secret, whereas privacy is concerned with keeping what *I* do secret (Lingel, Trammell, Sanchez, and Naaman 2012). But what does it mean for something to be secret?

Etymologically, the word *secret* came into use in the fifteenth century and is drawn from the Latin *secretus*, meaning "separated, divided"—in the context of dividing wheat from chaff (Prost and Vincent 1991, 63). In the basement community, secrecy endures as a form of separation, separating people who have access to information about basement music shows from those who do not. This separation does not occur incidentally or abstractly but rather through a set of decisions and norms that spring up around a given technology—what Henry Jenkins (2006) calls technological protocols.

In the next section, I discuss the various technological protocols of secrecy that are at work in the basement community. They emphasize flexibility (in a collective willingness to improvise and appropriate) and authenticity (in a commitment to local DIY and punk values and in shared concerns for determining authentic interests in the community). As a field study, the basement community allows us to think about the ways that countercultural spaces themselves are reshaped by commitments to secrecy and to explore the sociotechnical assemblages that have emerged to support the punk scene. In contrast to the fixity and top-down organization of technologies like Facebook, the basement community values flexibility and fluidity, which are visible in the physical structures of show spaces as well as collective practices of communicating online.

Sociotechnical Tactics of Basement Secrecy

As is described at the start of this chapter, New Brunswick's basement community has developed distinct practices that shape how, when, and where music shows take place. Although I had participated in punk communities for many years, New Brunswick punk shows felt different to me because it was immediately apparent that a distinct set of rules governs the interactions between the show hosts, fans, bands, and performance spaces. The community's rules are tied to members' concerns about avoiding detection of shows by law enforcement agencies. Lacking all but the most rudimentary sound-control tactics, basement performances are often very loud, thereby risking noise violations. Alcohol circulates freely at shows, exposing the hosts to potential charges for facilitating underage drinking. A show's attendance can range from four or five people to dozens, and participants described receiving warnings from fire marshals about the danger of large crowds in basements that typically have only one exit route. The tacit acceptance of smokers at shows—particularly given the use of objects like mattresses, newspapers, and packaging materials to muffle sound—further increases possibility of charges stemming from fire code violations. The threat of law enforcement does not always come directly. Disapproving show-house landlords who learn about performances might use the prospect of police and fire marshal sanctions to discourage future shows or even threaten eviction.

The above factors contribute to basement enthusiasts' perception that they are under constant surveillance, which they attempt to disrupt in how they use digital technologies like social media. The following brief account describes the key online platforms that are used to circulate information about New Brunswick basement music shows as organizers simultaneously promote shows to fans and attempt to dodge police interventions. I also list some offline tactics that are used to keep shows secret, such as reworking basement spaces to meet community needs. From there, I turn to the rules and norms that guide flows of information, including tactics for occluding addresses of shows and attempts to evaluate whether requests for information come from police officers or community members. All of these practices reflect the community's commitment to DIY values and its dual investment in flexibility and authenticity as the guiding principles for keeping insiders informed and outsiders excluded.

Online Platforms

New Brunswick's basement punk music community is dominated by young people. As is the case for many young adults, New Brunswick punks use a range of online platforms and mobile devices in their everyday lives, most of which they also use for their interactions within the basement community. The two social media sites most frequently referenced during interviews were Facebook and Myspace. One focus group participant listed flyers and texting as tools of communication and then admitted, "To be honest, even more than flyers I use Facebook. I invite all my friends who normally come, and then through that they can invite everyone to the Facebook event too." Even as participants often criticized the site as mainstream and capitalist, they also expressed resignation about their dependence on Facebook invites and fan pages to communicate about shows. The prevalence of Facebook use among members of their target audience made avoiding it all but impossible.

Although Myspace no longer enjoys the widespread popularity of now-dominant Facebook, the platform still had a significant presence in 2010, particularly among the indie bands that dominate New Brunswick basement shows. As one participant claimed in a 2010 interview, "If a show wasn't listed [on Myspace], people just wouldn't go. People would go, 'Oh, I didn't know about it.'" However, as far back as my initial interviews in 2009, participants saw Myspace as less important than Facebook for circulating information about the community and were dismissive of the platform's general relevance even as they acknowledged that many local bands and some show houses maintained Myspace profiles. By 2015, the platform had nearly dropped out of the social media landscape. A third social networking service used by the basement community is Reddit. Although the site was rarely mentioned by participants, I found a healthy discussion of New Brunswick's music scene in which bands posted about upcoming shows and addressed queries about the history and politics of the community.[2]

In addition to the mainstream online platforms described above, several online message boards have hosted discussions of the local music scene.[3] Some have been active for years, while others only emerged recently. According to interviewees, these sites were used for a range of activities, including archiving show flyers, discussing recent releases of albums, and posting information about upcoming basement shows. Message boards marked one of the key distinctions between long- and short-term members of the scene, with longtimers using them much more often than short-timers, who were often unaware of message boards. This reflected in part my use of snowball sampling. Because several participants were friends with each other, when one of them used a message board, the rest soon followed, and the message board became a way of maintaining friendships.

Offline Tactics of Secrecy

In addition to digital technologies, the New Brunswick basement music community has developed other tools of secrecy that I describe briefly to provide a richer description of how it feels to participate in the community's nightlife. Understanding these offline tactics provides a broader context for examining the community's relationship to technology in terms of secrecy.

Insulation

Most of the basements being used as music show spaces in the New Brunswick area are informally soundproofed to reduce the noise of live performances. Show-house residents use a variety of materials to create a layer of insulation around the perimeter of basement interiors. As one participant (and show-house resident) explained, "You can get free priority [U.S. Post Office mailing] boxes—like five hundred free priority boxes. If you stack them against the wall, they trap all the sound waves, especially the bass." Another participant noted that the basement location and the audience itself offer the most effective soundproofing: "The only real good soundproofing is … the basement. … The house that just got condemned: the basement was fully underground. Also people: like, if there's a lot of people in a basement, that will stop sound more than anything."

Stay off the Porch

Basement show hosts face the challenge of keeping audience and band members either inside the basement or in the backyard during shows, which helps to maintain the illusion that the house is "normal" rather than a site for live music performances. This tactic is important because punks who loiter in front of a house are a clear tipoff for any patrolling police

Figure 4.1
From a 2010 Screaming Females show. Note that the basement walls are lined with mattresses to provide sound insulation. Photo credit: Aaron Trammell.

officers that an illegal show is being held in the house. One participant who lived in a show house explained, "The backyard is a good thing. Our house doesn't have one, so we have to yell at people nonstop for people to stay off the front porch so the police don't file."

10 pm

Unusually for most live music events, basements shows in New Brunswick end early, typically before 10 pm. Several participants joked that while "punk time" generally refers to people or events running late, in New Brunswick it reflects a tendency toward punctuality. A common belief among show promoters was that New Brunswick's noise ordinance rules do not go into effect until 10 pm, although participants differed on the specifics of rule enforcement. Whether because of concerns that the noise ordinance will be enforced or that neighbors are more likely to report loud noises to the police after a certain time, show promoters typically choose to begin and end shows early. An excerpt from the focus group discusses the evolution of the 10 pm ending time:

Richard: I don't even know if it's true, but [I heard that] after 10 the noise violation ticket goes up [in cost].

Metal: Not true. To get rid of the frat on College Ave. [a main street in the middle of campus], they made it a twenty-four-hour noise violation. You can get it at any time.

McCoy: It's just kind of a logic thing. People that would be prone to call the cops probably wouldn't call them until 9:30 or 10 o'clock.

Many of these practices are likely to be familiar to anyone who has held band practices at their home or repeatedly hosted house parties in a residential area, although the above tactics were much more consistently (and stringently) enforced at shows I attended than they are at most house parties.

The New Brunswick basement community has developed some less familiar tactics related to avoiding detection of shows by local authorities. Arguably the most singular mechanism for avoiding police detection involves treating house addresses as secret. As Tim explained, "The information that's exchanged is basically when, how much, and who's playing. Never a where." Two distinct models emerged for keeping this information secret—code names and "ask a punk."

Code Names and "Ask a Punk"

During my fieldwork, I noted a shift in how information was exchanged about upcoming shows, reflecting the idea that practices of secrecy are ongoing and adaptable (Dourish et al. 2004, 328). During the first year that I attended basement shows, houses were referred to by code names rather than by addresses. Predictably, these code names often mentioned punk or obscure cultural references (for example, the Gutter, Ramones House, and the Bread Box). Lacey described the rationale for code names as follows: "I think [code names] are very necessary just because of cops. Cops like breaking up shows, and we don't want cops at our shows." Code names allow members of the punk community to rechristen houses as firmly entrenched punk locales, where names perform local identity and provide a measure of security. Eventually, however, the community suspected that local police had become aware of the house code names, and the ask-a-punk model emerged.

Figure 4.2
From a 2010 Screaming Females show. As a local band that was gathering increasing national attention, Screaming Females drew a large crowd. This photo shows a crowded venue where spectators see very little of the band, even though it is only a few feet away from them. Photo credit: Aaron Trammell.

"Ask a punk" refers to the replacement of code names on promotional materials with the direction to ask a punk for information regarding show locations. Ask a punk replaces disguise through pseudonyms with the direct intervention of a human gatekeeper. Lowell confirmed the shift to the new model: "A lot of places have stopped using the code name and have started using ask a punk. ... There's only one other house I can think of that uses a code name ... so I think the code name thing is going out." Brady explained further: "Recently, people stopped even giving their houses' names 'cause a lot of people believed cops even found out about that. I don't know how true that is. So a lot of times now it just says, 'Ask me for address,' or, like, 'Email this for address.'" Tim, a longtime member of the community, described changes in information practices over the years: "In 1999, we would have no problem putting up the whole address on a flyer. Now you can't do that. A lot of the times, it has to do with the flyer just says 'Ask someone' where the show is." Increased security is ascribed to the ask-a-punk model over code names, as Midori suggested: "I think actually [a friend's] house is now 'Ask a punk.' That's their technical house title. But now everyone just uses it. It's just more security, more secretive that way."

Having most recently attended shows in spring 2015, I found that both ask a punk and code names were used but with the added twist that a code name now referred to a number of physical locations—perhaps the most literal demonstration of flexibility that I encountered at this field site. These multiple locations were typically clustered close together, with shows alternating between houses operating under the same name. The expansion of code names to include several sites was a display of flexibility, but the tactical transition more broadly reflected the basement community's commitment to flexibility—that is, to manage strategic obstacles to communication by shifting practices of communication.

In terms of how these tactics play out online, organizers inform their networks of fans and bands about upcoming events on Facebook, which is widely understood as a critical promotional tool. However, the platform's utility reaches its limit when it comes to show addresses. It is not necessarily impossible to find secure ways of using Facebook, but it is generally perceived as being insecure. Unlike text messaging, which is felt to be a safe method of communicating privileged information, events that are posted on Facebook are treated as unsafe. Rules against listing show house addresses also are maintained on message boards. To find the address, potential audience members are required to contact the band's or the show's organizers, typically by direct messaging on Facebook, texting, or face-to-face communication.

After participating in punk and indie music scenes elsewhere, I was initially taken aback by the extensive measures that the New Brunswick community took to control local flows of information. Their protocols contradicted a basic premise of event promotion—that show information should be as accessible as possible to draw the largest possible audience to an event. Instead of eliminating hurdles to entry in a bid to attract more people, a New Brunswick basement norm was to erect sociotechnical barriers to inclusion. With all of the tactics described here for keeping shows secret (but particularly the practices of code names and ask a punk), there is a tension of exclusivity versus publicity, echoing the membership tensions

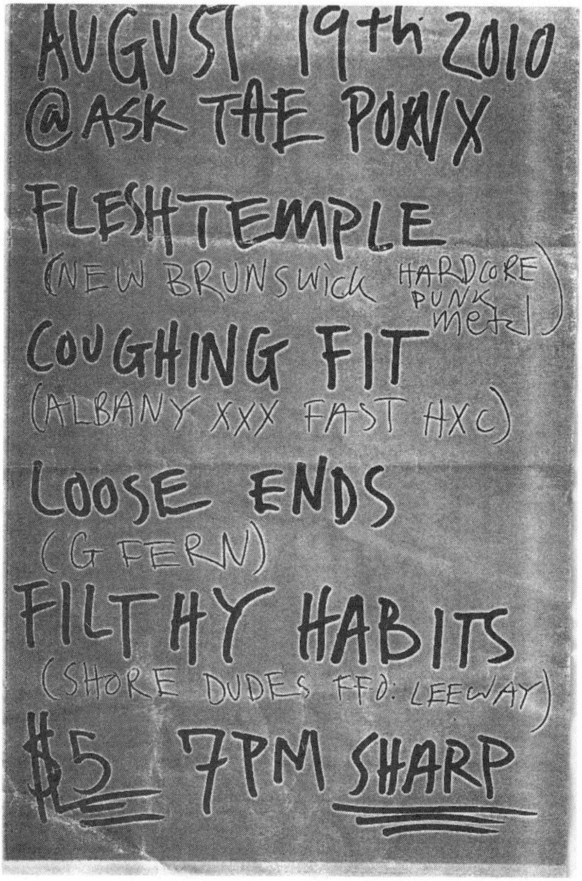

Figure 4.3
A flyer from a 2010 basement show. Note that the time, cost, and bands are listed but that the location says only "Ask the punx."

described in the previous chapter. A key difference between BME and New Brunswick is the taken-for-grantedness of membership attrition. The community's proximity to Rutgers University means that there is a predictable turnover in participants. Membership turnover results in a continual process of enculturating newcomers by exposing them to the fine line between committed community secrecy and arbitrary social exclusivity. In a small community that did not have a constant flow of potential new members, it would be more problematic to insist on rigid information practices, and there would be consequences for excluding people arbitrarily. But with a steady supply of new people to the area, New Brunswick punks have—to some extent—the luxury of embracing exclusivity.

Participants voiced varying degrees of concern about the community's exclusivity. Referring to ask a punk, Brady said, "I don't think it's supposed to be like, 'Hey you're not punk. You don't know anything.' It's not discriminating against anybody. It's just a little phrase that became the thing to put on a flyer." Brady's comment both highlights the transitory nature of information practices ("It's just a little phrase that became the thing") and downplays the possibility of alienation ("It's not discriminating against anybody"). Tim expressed a similar view: "There's no one walking around like, 'Oh, I was going to go to that show, but I didn't know where it was.' That never happens."

Brady's and Tim's comments reflect long-timers' perspectives on the scene, but others had difficulty finding a show's location, even if they knew the date, time, and names of the bands that were playing. For example, Lowell described his experience: "So when I first moved here, I would go to Myspace, and I would search the New Brunswick zip code to see if there was anything going on. And then from there, there would be a struggle to find an address because I didn't know where anything was because this was when I first moved down here. I didn't know any code names. I didn't know anyone really. I just tried to figure it out." This description illustrates how social media sites enable outsiders to access some (but not all) of the information that is required for show attendance. Mahdu offered a more measured view of the possible effects of ask a punk on the scene's inclusivity: "I thought it was the dumbest thing ever at first. People were like, 'Ask someone where the show is,' and I was like, 'Well, that's stupid because why should I have to go out of my way to find out where the show is?' And I did it, 'cause I wanted to go to these shows, but then I realized that it's important that we keep what we do a secret." Even if they were initially dubious of the necessity for tactical secrecy, participants often said they were willing to adhere to these practices due to community pressure, which was most frequently justified by the need to evade police.

Legitimate Secrecy: Cops and Noobs

Throughout the basement community, there is a widely held belief that the local police are committed to shutting down punk shows. One fear, which was related to online practices of secrecy, was that the police were using social media sites to obtain show information. As described by Tim: "Somebody on the police force made a Myspace page saying that this was going to be the official New Brunswick punk scene Myspace page and they wanted you to send them all the shows that were coming up so that they could post them—kind of like posing as someone in the punk scene." Mahdu related a similar experience:

> Cops have definitely contacted me before, trying to figure out where shows are. I won't email them back. If I get an email from someone, I always search their email on Facebook or Myspace, cause a lot of times, it'll come up "Not found." I don't email them. If I see that it's a kid, I'll email them. If I see that it's not a kid—'cause you wouldn't believe how many dumb cops there are; their email is just whatever they have on Facebook—I'll email them back like, "Sorry, show's canceled." I'll just tell them that the show is canceled. That's happened a lot of times.

In this instance, Facebook is used not to share information but to evaluate requests for information and determine whether requesters are police officers or newcomers.[4] The legitimacy of an information request is tested through ad hoc sociotechnical norms that lead show organizers to evaluate the legitimacy of a query based on social and linguistic cues that the request is legitimate (from a punk) or illegitimate (from the police). Message boards enjoy a small but dedicated following in the basement community, partly because participants feel that the police are not aware that the boards exist. As Matt pointed out: "We know that we can trust [that the boards are] being read by thirty different people and none of them are cops."

Given the regularity with which this suspicion of law enforcement infiltration was expressed, I asked participants how basement community members determined that an inquiry from a stranger was not genuine. Responses emphasized displays of social capital and local knowledge. For example, in a 2011 interview, Matt described an online encounter with someone he believed was an impostor:

> The profile was new. There weren't any pictures of the person on it. They had like five friends. ... And it was just strange. You know, like the old Supreme Court definition of *pornography*: like, I can't say what it is, but I know what it is when I see it. It was like that. There was really no one thing in particular that was, like, "Oh, caught you red-handed." It was just uncomfortable.

The community's awareness of various information practices and social protocols (some of which involved granular and subjective displays of language and vernacular) provided metrics for inclusion, which in turn produced a collective sense of comfort.

The ask-a-punk model itself is a ritualized information practice that signals membership within the community. Madhu, a longtime participant and band member, questioned whether the need for such rituals was more manufactured than necessary: "I think some people embrace the sexiness of the whole thing—like, 'Oh, man, the cops are on our ass, [but] we gotta do this show.' It's really juvenile, but I think some people find a romanticism in that." Regardless of whether Mahdu's doubts are well founded, the community's implementation of this particular ritual of secrecy contributes to the establishment of social norms, allowing members to gain or maintain cultural capital and inclusion in the counterculture.

New Brunswick's sociotechnical tactics for ensuring secrecy developed pragmatically out of the need to avoid the attention of law enforcement, but the practices have two additional objectives that relate to alterity and authenticity. First, by setting up an us-versus-them division, New Brunswick punks position themselves in continual opposition to local authorities, who are powerful symbols of the enforcement of mainstream norms of behavior, and this supports the basement community's sense of alterity. DIY ethics also matter here, in that the decentralized, horizontal networks that sustain the basement community contrast sharply with the strong tendency toward hierarchy and vertical command structures that is found in institutions like the police.

Second, threats of police intervention allow community members to exclude people that they simply might not like or want in the community. Like most countercultural movements, punk has been critiqued for reproducing the same strategies of exclusion and discrimination that it was originally intended to subvert. Laura Portwood-Stacer (2013) notes that anarchist groups often struggle to avoid setting up interpersonal hierarchies of substantive versus superficial commitment to anarchist values, sometimes determined by fairly shallow indications (such as how someone is dressed or what foods she eats). Similar to the ways that hairstyles, clothing, and demeanor have long characterized punk aesthetics (Hebdige 1995), fluency in locally accepted social media practices is required for obtaining online information about New Brunswick's underground network of shows. With resonances to BME in the previous chapter, tensions of membership emerge around whether practices of secrecy are unnecessary, counterproductive, overly restrictive, or inconsistent with DIY ethics of inclusion and participation.

All of the practices described here are tactical, in that they have arisen as flexible solutions to everyday problems through playful improvising within institutional(izing) structures. Indeed, sociotechnical tactics of secrecy in the basement community can be reframed entirely in terms of strategies and tactics—where alcohol licenses, event permits, and neighborhood noise ordinances are viewed as prohibitive strategies and where DIY insulation projects, early show times, and secretive practices of information exchange are viewed as tactics of resistance. For Michel de Certeau (1984), the construct of tactics is a useful way to theorize everyday life in terms of maintaining individual identity within dominant, mainstream culture. De Certeau was interested in daily acts of resistance from hegemonic institutions of state control, which he viewed as both ubiquitous and totalizing. For the basement community, the constant specter of police intervention has led to a shared culture of secrecy about where shows take place and a tendency toward exclusivity about who can obtain some kinds of knowledge.

Concerns of police detection were voiced so consistently within the community that some participants questioned the extent to which the fear of police detection was rooted in a legitimate threat and suggested that the tactics of secrecy actually were based on a romanticized construct that reinforced a sense of marginalization and alterity. Even if police detection was not as much of a threat as participants typically perceived, the police are still a symbol of (capitalist, hegemonic) authority and in that sense critical to understanding the community's tactics of secrecy.[5] The DIY and punk culture's anti-industry, anticapitalist values are deeply ingrained and are made visible in the basement community's antipolice rhetoric and the tactics that it used to control flows of information. These tactics also play a role in the realm of the personal, affecting aspects of community life such as individual judgment calls about whether and with whom to share information.

Upending Protocols: Consequences for Violating Basement Norms

The New Brunswick basement community's deep commitment to DIY ethics has given rise to particular sociotechnical tactics for managing information. But other than the threat of police detection, why would community members adhere to a somewhat onerous set of norms for communication? And what are the stakes for violating these tactics? To address these questions, I compare two breakdowns of community norms of secrecy that demonstrate the social and technological ramifications of subverting or setting aside existing practices. The first example involves a basement newcomer, Tom, who attempted to aggregate information about shows into a single online source and in doing so found himself ostracized from the basement community. The second example examines the decision to publicize a benefit show called Hub City Hardcore Fest (HCHF) to raise money for a community member's medical bills. When the police used online tools to investigate the concert—tracking down the exact location of show houses in the process—the community responded with a renewed commitment to tactics of secrecy. Tom's website is an example of an individual who transgresses against group norms and subsequently is disciplined by the community. HCHF is an example of community members who violate their own cultural norms, with lasting repercussions for the community's technological protocols. Both examples illustrate the technological limits of secrecy and reveal the crucial role of social norms and structures in countercultural communities.

The Limits of Sharing: Newcomer Missteps

Tom came to Rutgers University as an undergraduate, and as a fan of indie and punk music he was interested in attending local live shows. Because he was neither in a band nor a resident of a show house, Tom's access to information about basement performances was at first limited, similar to the experience of other newcomers. Tom eventually met a classmate who was involved in the community and started taking him to shows. After a few months, Tom grew frustrated with the limitations of relying on a single individual to obtain information and decided to circumvent existing tactics of information control by creating a website that provided show information. As Tom described it, "I decided that I was going to take it into my own hands and see if I could get some new kids there." For Tom, one consequence of information control was that as a group, the basement community felt homogeneous and unvaried. This supports my earlier point that the tactics of secrecy that are developed to avoid police detection also contribute to exclusivity, allowing for the expression of personal bias in determining who looks "punk enough" to become involved in the community.

Tom's website preserved the basement scene norm of not providing addresses for houses and listed only upcoming shows by date, time, band name, and house code name. He explained, "That would be enough for someone to be, like, able—if they really wanted to go to a show—[to] find the name of the house, ask a kid, whatever. At least they had a starting point, so they could, you know, go experience the show." Despite the fact that addresses were withheld, preserving a core technical element of basement tactics, Tom's website lacked adequate countercultural credentials and generated hostile reactions. Tom related an incident in which punk community members confronted him at a basement show, saying, "You don't have permission to do this. Why are you doing this?" The comments were accompanied by threats of physical violence and forcible removal from shows. This anecdote points to both a hierarchical structure (permission) and a lack of inclusiveness (epitomized by threats of excommunication from the community).

The negative responses to Tom's site were due in part to his insufficient reputation in the basement punk scene—what Sarah Thornton (1996) would call subcultural capital. Adapting Pierre Bourdieu's (2011) work on cultural capital and doing extensive fieldwork with club kids and ravers in England led Thornton to develop an analysis of how members of underground music scenes use insider knowledge to signal their belonging within a group. Tom's intervention would likely have found some sympathy from others who felt that the basement community was overly strict in its practices of information control. But although the ends of his website might have been welcome to some, the means of implementation lacked evidence of adequate subcultural capital. I read Tom's website as an intrusion into existing practices, so when longtime members of the community evaluated his implied criticism of the status quo, they felt that he lacked adequate capital within the local community to intervene in its practices.

Another and related factor was that Tom acted alone in a community whose DIY values stressed collaborative deliberation and bottom-up decision making. As a relative newcomer to the scene, Tom's actions were met with suspicion. He stated that he had "a lot of trouble because people … [didn't trust me] having this information." Without layers of trust built through extended time in the community, Tom lacked local support for his project and could not figure out how to get it. He eventually took down the site, and although he continued to go to shows on occasion, he always felt like an outsider in the community. The dismantled site remained up for several years, blank except for a single line of text: "Ask punk kids where to find shows." Ironically, these instructions essentially reinforce the same information practices that Tom initially set out to challenge.

The Limits of Mutual Aid: The Failure of Hub City Hardcore Fest

In summer 2009, members of the New Brunswick basement music community organized a series of benefit shows that collectively were labeled Hub City Hardcore Fest (HCHF) to raise funds for a community member who was diagnosed with cancer. Festival organizers prioritized their objective of raising money and decided to set aside existing norms of secrecy. Presale tickets were sold online, the addresses of the basement venues were printed on each ticket, and the event was covered in local newspapers and websites. As a result, the local police soon became aware of the shows. In some ways, HCHF reveals what happened when the basement community attempted to operate formally rather than informally, above ground rather than underground.

Well before the scheduled date of the benefit performances, problems arose for HCHF organizers. Police officers who previously were unable to locate show houses purchased tickets online as a way to identify the residences that were being used as illegal venues. One research participant explained: "The cops bought all of the tickets to get all of the addresses. So now they had the name of the house and the address, and that fucked everyone."

Taking preventative measures, the police contacted the landlords of houses where the promoters planned to host shows and promised citations if the shows continued. Alarmed landlords threatened their tenants with eviction, which brought HCHF planning efforts to a halt. In an effort to salvage what was left of the festival, organizers consolidated the performances into a single event and relocated to the Court Tavern (the only eighteen-and-over venue in town). Audience confusion over the changes, the costs of securing the new venue, and the general timbre of police awareness resulted in decreased revenue for the benefit, deepening the organizers' frustration. Beyond the event itself, the breach in information practices temporarily put basement shows on hiatus while community members waited for police attention to be diverted elsewhere. Show organizers attempted to recuperate stability through a renewed commitment to word-of-mouth rather than online communication networks, a defensive move toward tactics of keeping information secret and holding newcomers in suspicion.

Tom's website failed because it violated implicit norms of social control, even as he included the explicit mechanisms of information control that had been established by community standards. His exclusion and ostracization resulted not because he had information but because he tried to disseminate information in a way that was in conflict with the cultural norms of the basement community. In the case of HCHF, collective secrecy practices were violated within the community itself in an effort to pursue a common economic goal. Although that goal was consistent with the DIY value of mutual aid, the project fell short of success when organizers departed from the community's secrecy norms and then found themselves unable to shield show houses from police detection.

Both Tom's encounter with community resistance and the community's return to word-of-mouth promotion after it used public information channels for a charity event are examples of community self-policing in the face of (real or perceived) threats of police intervention. Online technologies did not introduce tensions of secrecy and surveillance to this countercultural community, but they did sharpen the contours of decision points surrounding the social and technological practices of secrecy.

Conclusions

Given that New Brunswick, New Jersey, is home to a large university, it is not surprising that an active community of young people supports local live entertainment. What *is* surprising are the technologies and online platforms that are deployed within this community as part of its commitment to localized values of secrecy. We tend to think of young people as fluent in and dependent on digital media for self-expression and social connection (although the inaccuracies of this logic are well documented: see boyd 2014 and Vaidhyanathan 2008). New Brunswick's basement community provides an example of young people who have collectively committed to using social media in a way that often involves personal inconvenience and technological redundancy. The payoff for committing to these tactics is a feeling of actively contributing to the long-term survival of local punk music.

Learning social norms and subsequently adhering to them is critical to membership in any group. In their research on risk in leisure groups, Gary Alan Fine and Lori Holyfield (1996, 28) argue that obtaining information, which requires both social and technical skills, is one of the first goals of group membership. Similarly, in New Brunswick's basement community, membership is about both access to information and fluency with information. By conforming to community norms of secrecy through tactics like code names and ask a punk, newcomers signal their shared values and countercultural savviness. Technology allows members to demonstrate their fluency in tactics of disseminating information appropriately (or in Tom's case, inappropriately), but technology can also allow members to determine whether a claim to community information is valid (as when several participants reported using platforms like Facebook to authenticate an unfamiliar name on message boards or in email requests for information about shows).

Community procedures for authentication point to what Elfreda A. Chatman (1999) calls the performative nature of information. In her work with inmates at a women's maximum security prison, Chatman (1999, 208) argues that information is "really a *performance*. It carries a specific *narrative* that is easily adaptable to the expectations and needs of members of a small world." Chatman's insight is to point out the ways that information is never just about content; it also is about context. Evaluating the usefulness of information is often a matter of whether information is valid, but Chatman adds the crucial point that interpreting information is also about the social context in which it is received and circulated—how it is performed. In the basement community, information is performed on flyers and Facebook invitations via code names and ask a punk, tactics that have taken shape within both larger narratives of DIY and punk values and the contingent narratives of secrecy. In addition to these communication performances, requests for information about basement shows are also evaluated in terms of whether they adequately perform localized norms.

Although the basement community's tactics for secrecy are rooted in avoiding threats of detection from the authorities, their methods of exclusion also support the community's interest in seeing itself as countercultural. As David Muggleton (2000, 63–64) notes in his work on secrecy, "invoking a reference group enables certain individuals to emphasize their 'insider' status as members of an esoteric scene through self-exclusion from a larger category of uninitiated 'outsiders.'" When New Brunswick punks invoke the police as a reference group in their commitment to secrecy, they set up a relationship to information that is performative, signaling their opposition to the police and mainstream rules of social behavior in general. In terms of how digital technologies support the basement community, the performative dimension of information, both online and off, becomes a way of operationalizing a collective commitment to DIY values.

Part of the performative nature of information and technology in the basement community relies on a backdrop of punk and DIY as countercultural identity. It also relies on a set of expectations about how young people use technology. Rather than tools of self-promotion and oversharing, platforms like Facebook and Reddit become media of secrecy, which Graham M. Jones (2014, 56) describes as "the vehicles through which relations of inclusion and exclusion or similarity and difference are modulated via communicative practices of concealment, revelation, revelation of concealment, and concealment of revelation." In this countercultural context, it is not just a matter of whether to use technologies but how to use them. Ben Light (2014) argues that simple binary of connecting and disconnecting does not do justice to the complexities of everyday online life, which tend to involve multiple platforms and profiles whose arrangements can change frequently.[6] Light's unpacking of the different assumptions that are embedded in touting connectivity resonate with New Brunswick punks' collective commitment to secrecy and their use of a range of technologies to meet a specific set of goals.

Returning to the three-part framework that I use throughout this book—legibility, flexibility, and authenticity—one way of thinking about the failure of Tom's website is that it lacked authenticity. Tom's interests in punk were sincere, but his objectives and his website were interpreted as illegitimate because he failed to follow existing social structures for information sharing. Basement punks did not see clear signals that their local values were embedded in the sites. Instead, they saw interference from an interloper. I have defined the word *secrecy* as fundamentally collective—a group commitment to protecting shared practices and activities. Because Tom acted alone rather than with others in the community, his website was doomed to be censured.[7] Although the information that he presented on his website was identical to that found at other sources, he lacked adequate enculturation to perform and narrate this information among his peers.

Although this chapter does not talk much about legibility, issues of legibility might have contributed to the demise of Tom's site. One problem was that community members rejected as inauthentic Tom's claims to information. A separate problem was that the community found it difficult to address Tom's newcomer information needs. Although Tom failed to solicit community feedback before acting, he was never clear about how he could have asked permission (and thus acted within the community's social and information norms). No legible structure was in place for adjudicating existing practices of information sharing or for requesting significant changes to information flows within the community. Tom's website brings into relief the risks of prioritizing secrecy over legibility—such as potentially alienating newcomers with genuine interests in the community and reinforcing structures of control and hierarchy that many countercultures seek to contest.

Participants invoked the example of the Hub City Hardcore Fest as a justification for practices of secrecy, but these tactics have important consequences. One is that these practices exclude people who have legitimate interests in punk but may simply not appear that way (online or off) to current community members. Another is that determining whether to share information stems from trying to avoid police detection of shows and can be a subjective decision. Community members can exclude others for personal or arbitrary reasons under the veil of adhering to values of protecting community viability. Questions of legitimacy surface across different countercultural tactics in this community—in deciding whether to use Facebook, Myspace, or text messages to distribute information about a show; in using norms of social media activity to determine whether someone is a cop or a newcomer; or in evaluating whether a technological intervention is welcome or grounds for ostracization. The differing mechanisms of performing and evaluating legitimate interests in New Brunswick punk demonstrate the limits of a purely technological approach to secrecy. Because membership in a countercultural community is socially determined, information that is made available only to members will always require social as well as technological determinations of access.

In some ways, the basement community's ability to enforce exclusivity through the various tactics of determining membership that are identified in this chapter can be seen as a luxury. Show organizers can afford to be selective about whom they invite—and how they invite them—because basement performances are so often (literally) the only show in town. The small, cramped nature of basements means that a show can feel full with just a dozen people. Although I've been to several underattended shows, I have also been to performances that felt uncomfortably crowded. It takes work to organize well-attended basement shows, but New Brunswick enjoys the advantage of a stable population of young people who have limited options for local entertainment. Moreover, young people are more likely to submit to the rigors of performing countercultural alterity than other age groups, simply because they lack access to other registers of status (such as having a family or a career, for example).[8]

A second characteristic of how technological alterity takes shape in the basement community relates to flexibility, where countercultural tactics adapt with emerging technologies and against shifting strategies of infiltration. Returning to Chatman's (1999, 208) point about information as performance, she writes that information "is easily adaptable to the expectations and needs of members of a small world." This reference to adaptability dovetails with my own emphasis on flexibility as a sociotechnical tactic that benefits communities of alterity. The basement community has expectations and needs (secrecy and ideological affiliation with punk and DIY values) that manifest in a shifting array of flexible tactics. Flexibility is valued in practices that reflect countercultural values (such as taking advantage of the DIY viewpoint that technologies are always subject to appropriation by insulating basements) as well as the adoption of new norms of codifying secret information (such as shifting from code names to ask a punk).

Online communication tactics are in many ways less flexible than their offline counterparts, in part because digital platforms themselves are leaky and easily subject to infiltration. It is easier for police to spend an hour fishing on Facebook than show up at shows disguised as punk rockers. Unlike basements themselves, the infrastructure of Facebook cannot be tweaked or modified, at least not at the immediate demands of New Brunswick punk enthusiasts. Unable to soundproof Facebook invites from unwelcome listening, the community relies on online communications without publicizing the most vulnerable information—the addresses of show houses. The practice of occluding addresses persists on sites where community members hold sway over design, like message boards and locally run show sites. Yet what is interesting to me is that despite the rhetoric of the Internet as endlessly adaptable and programmable—evident in dogmatic statements like "information wants to be free" and the emphasis on participatory media—for countercultural communities that seek to keep secrets about their activities and maintain their sense of alterity, online platforms can feel frustratingly inflexible.

The New Brunswick basement community demonstrates how even inflexible platforms that come with known security risks can be fit into a wider assemblage of technologies and practices and become flexible through technological protocols and collective appropriation. Instead of rejecting mainstream information and communication technologies wholesale, members of the basement community rely on collectively honed tactics of secrecy to leverage the convenience of online communication without entirely sacrificing security. As a community, New Brunswick punk persists partly because of local factors (a steady supply of university students, a physical proximity to New York and Philadelphia, a paucity of local venues to hear live music) and partly through the collective adoption of and commitment to sociotechnical tactics of secrecy.

5 Fight for Your Platform to Party: Brooklyn Drag and the Battle for a Queerer Facebook

In the religion of drag queens, the high holidays are Halloween and New Year's Eve. In Brooklyn, there is also Bushwig, arguably the city's most anticipated drag event of the year. Although the two-day festival has moved from its original home in Bushwick, Brooklyn, to a new location in Ridgewood, Queens, the key components are the same—tents, stages, and dozens of high-heeled drag queens with meticulously applied makeup. Alternately nervous and excited, performers line up near the stage for their turn at a one-song set, which typically involves lip synching and dancing, in genres that can vary from hip-hop to pop to polka. Fans and spectators—queer and straight, mostly young, many dressed up so elaborately that they are indistinguishable from the performers onstage—mill around in the late summer heat, drinking beer, evaluating costumes and routines, and occasionally hooking up. Since 2012, the festival has been many things—a sensory overload of glitter, drama, hair dye, and glamour; a victorious display of dance, comedy, irony, and farce. It also reflects Brooklyn's rapid transformation from a neighborhood dominated by light industry warehouses into one filled with coffee shops and bars. Importantly for drag culture, these changes accommodate not just a vibrant nightlife but a vibrant queer nightlife.[1]

Throughout the two days of the Bushwig, people snap photos of themselves and others, many of which will be uploaded to social media sites and disseminated across an international network of family, friends, fans, and followers. Within the local drag community, these media artifacts help individual performers to promote themselves and advertise upcoming shows. Although online networks now are commonly thought of as an audience (Litt 2012), for drag queens this is literally true. In addition to the work of making costumes and choreographing routines, drag queens undertake substantive work in their online performances, cultivating their fan bases by posting content and engaging with followers on social media.

Unlike the other two communities examined in this book, members of the Brooklyn drag community tend not to be interested in secrecy.[2] After all, the nature of drag is fundamentally expressive and hypervisible. But although the drag queens I interviewed were largely uninterested in keeping their community secret, this does not mean that information is uncontrolled. Brooklyn's drag queens are invested in taking advantage of social media platforms for both individual self-promotion and community support, benefits that help explain the ubiquitous use of Facebook and Instagram among performers. Yet the use of digital technologies comes with critiques of their potential for bias and discrimination, which drag queens associated with policies around names and queer identities.

In fall 2013, I interviewed members of Brooklyn's drag community with Adam Golub, a documentary filmmaker and queer activist. We conducted a series of focus groups with fifteen queens, asking them about the role that social media played in their lives as performers. We also took advantage of a two-day drag arts festival held in Manhattan in November 2013 to conduct a workshop (attended by approximately forty people) as a way of getting feedback on key themes that emerged from the focus groups. In fall 2015, I conducted a small number of follow-up interviews to ask about any changes that had occurred in the community since the first round of interviews. In particular, I wanted to understand how Brooklyn's drag community responded to Facebook's 2014 "real-name" policy, later called its "authentic-name" policy, which led to the freezing or shutting down of the accounts of hundreds of drag queens because they had used a name other than their legal name. I return to this controversy at the end of the chapter in my discussion of authenticity as a design value for communities of alterity.

In this third field study, I look at how drag queens as a countercultural community use and make sense of mainstream digital technologies like Facebook and also how such tools fail to accommodate the fluidity and complexities of their lives. Careful examination of this community's relationship to Facebook brings into relief a number of sociotechnical tensions that have been central to this book—between alterity and the mainstream, between the strategic and the tactical, and between the ways that technologies are designed and the ways that they are used in everyday life. By setting up comparisons between how Facebook and members of this community understand the concepts of authenticity and community, we can see the underlying logics that support some forms of identity work over others. I also work through different ways of thinking about and benefitting from community, particularly the gap between Facebook's claim to being a global community and the queerer and more countercultural community of drag queens.

Context: Brooklyn's Drag Renaissance

Typically, the word *drag* refers to a male-bodied performer who stages a hyperfeminized lip-synching of a female vocalist, often accompanied by dancing and comedy. Drag has a long history in New York, reflected in films such as *Paris Is Burning* and festivals like Wigstock, an annual drag extravaganza held in Manhattan in the 1980s and 1990s. In contemporary Brooklyn drag, the objective is rarely (or rarely just) female illusionism, which refers to a realistic and convincing performance of mainstream femininity. Instead, performers tend to be more interested in genderfucking and genderqueering or as one participant put it, being a "gender terrorist"—that is, playing with and disrupting conventional notions of femininity and masculinity.

Some examples from the Brooklyn drag scene can help to illustrate the distinction in these approaches to drag. I have seen an androgynous performer cover a Yeah Yeah Yeah's song, including a lengthy interruption of robotic yet maniacal laughter, which she sporadically interrupted by shooting a confetti gun; a male-bodied performer don a strap-on penis over her own penis and testicles, which had been taped to her thighs;[3] a drag ensemble satirize the transgendered villain from *Silence of the Lambs*, surrounded by goblins; and a drag queen dressed in Orthodox Jewish clothing, performing choreography that mimicked electrocution. These performances were not particularly invested in mainstream drag (as oxymoronic as that phrase may seem) but instead embraced a heterogeneous array of performance practices, stage personas, and sexualities. As described by one queen I interviewed: "We are not pageant queens. That's the cool thing about what's going on now. You can give what you want. You don't have to really box it in. You can just let go and deliver what you want to present, which is really beautiful." Another queen echoed this description: "I've been on the same bill as burlesque performers, twerkers—like, performance art that has nothing to do with drag as it is by the book, in terms of heels, hair, and makeup. The spirit, the intimacy of the scene is, I'd say, bigger than that. It's more inclusive than that. It's more performance oriented rather than fitting-into-the-mold oriented."

All of the participants that I interviewed lived in Brooklyn, and all but one lived in the neighborhood of Bushwick. Since about 2010, Brooklyn has hosted what could be called a drag renaissance, and the nexus of this renaissance is Bushwick. About 125,000 people live in Bushwick, and about 40 percent of them are from Puerto Rico or the Dominican Republic (U.S. Census Bureau 2010). Although not a historically queer neighborhood, today it is a nexus of relatively affordable housing, reliable transportation, and proximity to a thriving urban nightlife, which follows neighboring Williamsburg's trajectory of gentrification (Petrilli 2012). These factors have also supported an explosion in drag performances, as evidenced by an increase in the number of actively performing queens from four or five just a few years ago to approximately a hundred now (Bushwig 2014). At the time I was writing this book, live drag shows could be seen on any night of the week.

Drag as Queer Community

I have used the word *community* throughout this book, but the term takes on a particular valence in the context of queer identity and culture (Weston 1991). When drag queens embrace the term *community*, it has particular resonances (similar to the word *family*) of queer solidarity and mutual aid. Like people at the other two field sites that I investigated, when asked about their preferences for how to describe themselves, Brooklyn drag queens unanimously preferred *community*. As one participant explained:

> It's a community. There's a definite community where we get together. We'll go to each other's shows. We'll actually support each other. If anyone needs help in any way— If something drastically horrible happened, I'm sure I could text [another queen], and she would be there in a minute. It's something that you can act upon, whereas maybe *subculture* is just a phenomenon that happens to a demographic.

Social support is central in the above definition of *community*, whereas *subculture* (for this participant) refers to an interest-based phenomenon. The distinction that emerges here is partly about solidarity and mutual aid but also about action and commitment. In other words, this definition of *community* is practice-based: *community* refers to something that

Figure 5.1
Map of Bushwick. The black arrows denote the Brooklyn neighborhoods of North and South Bushwick, conventionally referred to as a single entity, Bushwick. Image from the 2013 American Community Survey Profile of New York. Retrieved from maps.nyc.gov/census.

people *do,* whereas *subculture* relates to demographics or something that people *are*. Describing community as a shared set of doing points to Étienne Wenger's (1998) term *community of practice* (referenced in chapter 1) and also connects to my overall interest in sociotechnical tactics. Defining *group* as "community" is partly about shared values and ethics and partly about shared practices, including shared practices for digital technologies.

With parallels to the other field studies discussed in this book, participants liked the word *community,* yet they were not always inclusive or free from interpersonal policing. Consider the following focus group conversation between a new member of the community, who relates experiences of competition and hostility, and two more experienced drag queens, who present the community as welcoming and playful:

Participant 1:	I like community.
Interviewer:	Yeah?
Participant 2:	I feel like it is a community. I don't feel like it's heavily competitive.
Participant 3:	Yeah.
Participant 2:	Or a playground.
Interviewer 1:	Playground? [Laughter]
Participant 1:	I feel, like, when I approached it, it was competitive—
Participant 2:	Not sure.
Participant 3:	—at first—
Participant 1:	No, you're right.
Participant 2:	Yeah.
Participant 3:	But it's, like, if you take the view—
Participant 2:	It was very supportive.
Participant 1:	When you get over, you know, once I got over [the first few weeks].
Participant 2:	Because we see each other all the time. We see each other everywhere.
Participant 3:	But it's nice to know that if you go somewhere, you're going to know someone. [Laughs]
Participant 2:	Yeah.
Participant 1:	Yeah, yeah absolutely. It's nice.

The starts and interruptions in this conversation stem partly from a key divergence in how much local status or history is required to feel that Brooklyn drag constitutes a community rather than a competition. The reality is that both perspectives are accurate. Even if Brooklyn's drag community resembles a playground in terms of aesthetic experimentation, community members can nonetheless engage in interpersonal politics that (purposefully or not) can hinder participation.

Social Media and Drag Practice

In describing prior field studies, I focused on alternative technologies (such as message boards and BME's IAM network) used by communities of alterity. This chapter is less concerned with countercultural technologies than it is with how members of a countercultural community adapt mainstream technologies like Facebook to meet their particular needs. Drag queens use a range of technologies in their lives as performers, including mobile phones, tools for body hair removal, sewing machines, and DJ equipment.

The drag performers I interviewed tended to operate within mainstream social media platforms rather than develop their own digital technologies. In Michel de Certeau's (1984) terms, they engaged in tactical practices within the strategic infrastructures of dominant social media platforms.

In interviews, I asked drag queens to list all the social media sites that in some way support their drag practices. Everyone used Facebook and Instagram, and far fewer used sites like Tumblr and Twitter (table 5.1). In the discussion that follows, I focus on Facebook, which was considered both a highly valuable tool and a source of contention. Instagram was seen as

Table 5.1

Platform	Number of participants (n = 15)
Facebook	15
Instagram	15
Twitter	7
Tumblr	5
Scruff	2
Pinterest	1
Vimeo	1
Grindr	1
YouTube	1
Linked In	1
Fet Life	1
Vine	1
Yelp	1

Instead of providing focus groups with a checklist of online platforms, I asked participants to list the social media sites that they used. This means that platform use is likely underreported for some of the less common sites (for example, more participants probably had YouTube and LinkedIn accounts but did not think to list them without prompting). Because of this self-reporting approach, some sites listed may not meet standard definitions of what constitutes a social network site (boyd and Ellison 2013). My intent was not to gather a statistically accurate dataset of online participation but rather to get a sense of which social media sites were considered most important to everyday life as a drag performer.

similarly necessary but more straightforward and did not provoke the same tensions of online identity work.

Building a Repertoire, Documenting a Journey

Social media sites are important tools for drag queens, both in terms of fans and fellow performers. Regarding the latter, social media allows newcomers (whether to Brooklyn or to the drag community) to forge social ties to existing community members and expose them to other users, events, and (less explicitly) social norms and values.

For example, one participant noted that tracing the social network of an established queen became an entry point to learning about the drag community:

> I went and found her on Facebook and stalked all the shows she had been to in the past week and all the ones that she was going to for the upcoming weeks and started going to those. Through finding those events on Facebook, I found the other queens that were going to events and looked at their pages and the events they were going to and through actually going to these events met more people. It was this back and forth, from in person to online, building bridges and furthering connections until I had both an online and an in-person network of connections and events that I knew about and was familiar with. That's why I'm here. If I hadn't been able to start on Facebook and initially find things that way, I wouldn't have had any idea where to even start.

In this account, Facebook articulated the social ties within the drag community and provided an aggregate calendar of events and performances, which became nodes of connection within the community.

Another participant described a similar path to developing ties within the drag community via Tumblr:

> Tumblr is specifically how I met a lot of people in this Brooklyn drag scene. She's not a drag queen, but I met [a local DJ] through Tumblr. Then through her, I sort of watched the branches move outward. I was meeting people who were involved in this performance art scene, made friends with them, and ended up going to performances.

Social media enables a vital process of "watch[ing] branches move outward," which participants described as far more useful than offline approaches for integrating into the drag community. In our interview, this participant also noted that Tumblr was especially conducive to her interests in drag because the site has a devoted following among people with historically marginalized sexualities (Renninger 2015). She felt that the tagging functionality of Tumblr facilitated interest-based convergences, noting that the platform "brings people together, who even though for all intents and purposes might run parallel to one another, don't really have that sort of thematic cinch."

Participants described social media as being essential to the process of developing social networks, including a specifically queer community: "Yeah, so [Facebook] helped me find that gay community that's out here, [and] along the road I fell into this group that slowly became a family, and a … community." Given the widespread penetration of social media sites among adults (nearly two-thirds have at least one social media account, according to Perrin 2015), it is not surprising that platforms like Facebook and Tumblr facilitate social connectivity. In fact, several participants described themselves as being dependent on social media for information and communication:

Participant 1: Without Facebook, there's a lot of people who wouldn't know about anything.

Participant 2: I wouldn't know about any of this.

Participant 1: You know where to go because you check Facebook invites. … At least, that's what I do. I'll get on that week and make a list of where I have to be this week because I'll remember via [Facebook]. I don't know how even to be anything without being able to get on the computer and look what everyone's doing and what's happening. You'd just have to guess.

As Facebook develops features and tools for communication, such as location check-in and video chat, it has become increasingly important in social and professional interactions. In interviews, drag performers struggled to imagine their lives without Facebook, even as they disagreed with some of its features and design.

Beyond connecting people to each other, social media sites produce representations of drag practices and personas. Commitment to drag requires practitioners to continue to develop new routines and costumes, and social media sites offer a valuable means for documenting these changes over time. As one queen noted, "In the context of doing drag, the best thing about Facebook is being able to have a live anthology of your work, your growth, your development. It's just that you can go back at any given moment and see where you started and see everything." Another participant agreed, noting that Facebook acted as an archive of her changing drag practice, reflecting shifts in costumes and increased skill in drag as an art form: "Everyone has a journey in their drag. Everyone looks very different when they start to where when they are now."[4] When I asked drag queens about photos and videos that were available through their online social networks, they talked about these videos as a source of inspiration and self-critique. One queen explained:

> Looking back at old pictures and studying them and looking at things that [are useful] because your makeup constantly changes. You have to try new things, and then you'll go back and look at things you liked or things that you [want to change]. I've done that a lot, where I've looked back and [seen] what's changed. Either I want to pull it back in, or I'm like, "Good thing that changed."

Performers who think of Facebook as an online "anthology" experience both short- and long-term gains. In an immediate sense, they can use social media to self-promote and solidify social ties with their fan base and with other performers. In the long term, drag queens are able to catalog their routines and costumes, which becomes an important resource for developing their evolving stage personas.

In addition to archiving and learning from their own performances, participants used Facebook to track and study the evolution of other performers. One focus group participant described using Instagram to teach herself how to "paint," referring to the application of the heavy makeup required for her routines:

> It's a game I play. I'll go on Instagram and enter a hashtag [related to drag]. Then I have a rule. Whoever comes up—whatever queen it is, famous or not famous or whatever—I'll study her face and try to match her makeup exactly. And of course, it always comes out looking totally different. But that's how I challenge myself to learn new skills.

Similar to the way that YouTube serves as a source of ad hoc, how-to guides, social media offers queens a means of DIY instruction, allowing for informal knowledge sharing of makeup, styling, and choreography that supplements in-person mentorship (for example, having a drag "mother" who takes new performers under her wing). As a whole, social media offer the benefits of increased connectivity, personal archiving, and online skill sharing.

The online archiving of drag performances and culture is sustained largely by audience members who are armed with smartphones and social media accounts, and participants generally assumed that their live performances would generate digital artifacts that could later be circulated through Instagram and Facebook. Online audiences included their fans as well as other queens, and many performers I interviewed were invested in maintaining control over the media representations that surface from their performances: "I don't set it up for a photographer to be there, but you can be assured that when I get home, after I take the face off, I'm on Instagram—like, searching every hash tag possible and praying there's a good photo." I observed this work of culling through social media documentation in the days following the Bushwig festival, when performers were involved in a flurry of back-and-forth Facebook posts as they tracked down the best videos and photos of their performances.

Social media curation work is particularly important in the context of self-promotion. Just as social media connections enabled newcomers to gain entry into the Brooklyn drag community, an ongoing social media presence allowed performers to maintain connections to their online audiences. One participant described her commitment to maintaining a separate Facebook account for her drag persona:

> It's claiming a presence a little bit, connecting, mostly having some place where people can go because you meet people out in the nightlife. But the second you leave that bar, [my drag persona is] done. She actually gets washed down the drain, and I go to bed. But in the morning, people are still going to remember [her because of Facebook].

Drag queens are in face only during performances. In everyday life, most participants move through the world as gay men. In this sense, social media representations are more permanent than the events themselves, providing a record of drag performances that long outlives the live version.

Social media sites are a core technology in Brooklyn's drag community. The drag queens that I interviewed valued these platforms as a key resource for documenting past performances and planning future ones. The circulation of images and videos from drag performances also matters for promoting events and connecting drag performers to their fans and other drag performers. These drag performers could not imagine their community without the support of social media platforms, but they felt dependent on Instagram, YouTube, and particularly Facebook, which produced a set of concerns about the role that these technologies played within the community. In addition to experiencing a general sense of fatigue with mainstream digital technologies, participants described a tension between their identities as drag performers and Facebook as a platform that they perceived as monolithic, inflexible, and straight.

Fatigue Sets In: The Platform That Drag Queens Love to Hate

Interviewees voiced a sense of fatigue with Facebook and digital technologies in general, expressing exasperation about feeling obligated to be online to participate in the drag community. For example, one queen commented, "I love technology, but I have issues with it. I feel like it's made people become robots in a way. You go anywhere, and everyone's like [making texting sounds], just not talking. I guess it's just a sign of the times, but I miss human interaction." Despite their often sensational and exotic drag personas, participants often felt that it was too difficult to stand out in a crowded Facebook newsfeed. As one participant explained, "I do create events for [upcoming shows], but now everyone and their mother is invited to fifteen events a day. It's hard. I don't look at my events. I miss a lot of things just because I'm unaware of it now." In an online market for attention that is saturated with invites and updates from friends, family, coworkers, and casual acquaintances, even drag queens struggled to capture attention. Participants also expressed fatigue with both sending and receiving Facebook invites, even as they genuinely valued the ties that they had formed online. Social media practices of self-promotion often felt mandatory, a necessary means for staying connected to their fans and each other. At the same time, these performers were very aware of competition for attention, not just from other queens but from the platform as a whole.

In addition to feelings of exasperation and fatigue with constant social media use, participants reported that Facebook was a source of drama and interpersonal tensions (not unlike IAM's terms of service forum). Interpersonal drama tracked largely between individual performers, whereas online social support was exchanged between performers and fans. One participant explained: "I feel like a lot of people are really shady, especially on Facebook. I feel like when it comes from certain artists to artists, it's really just shade. But when it comes from a genuine supporter, it's always going to be positive." Based on an analysis of drag performers' Facebook use, there was no shortage of drama between the queens that I friended, with people mounting attacks and staging defenses as a regular feature of feeds and public messages. But this is the case for any online community, from high school friends (Marwick 2014) to feminist activists (Clark forthcoming). In the drag queen community, however, drama often plays a particular countercultural function.

Much like the mainstreaming of body modification (discussed in chapter 3), drag culture has been increasingly exposed to a mainstream (i.e. straight and white) audience. Thanks to television shows like *RuPaul's Drag Race*, parts of drag culture have been picked up in popular conversation, particularly the words *shade* and (to a lesser extent) *read*. The word *shade* refers to passive-aggressive hostility directed at another person or event, and *reading* refers to the back-and-forth, antagonistic exchange of insults between two drag queens (Livingston, Gibson, and Oppenheim 2005). Both terms derive from black street culture, in which drag balls and vogueing have their roots. When I was conducting fieldwork in 2013 and 2015, people far outside the community were using terms like *shade* to refer to anything from an incorrect bar tab to a political candidate's debate performance. Given the near-ubiquitous use of social media platforms among drag performers, it is not surprising that shade transpires online. As one participant put it: "There is a lot of friendship, but it's queens. Everyone's a bit catty sometimes. Nightlife by nature is that way."

Any qualitative accounting of Brooklyn's drag community (and probably any drag community) needs to acknowledge the role that shade plays in interpersonal communication between queens—a backstage counterpart to the onstage performances. Given the importance of social media within Brooklyn's drag community, it is inevitable that interpersonal tensions will surface on Facebook walls and Instagram posts. Yet the most critical comments I heard from participants about social media had little to do with users of Facebook and everything to do with Facebook's policies for how people should display their names and identities online.

In addition to exasperation and fatigue with social media, some participants expressed hesitation regarding the community's reliance on social media as a form of documentation. With a blend of anxiety and resignation, they described Facebook as imperfect but inescapable:

> Facebook is, like, all we have anymore, too, though. To create an archive [of our community], it's all we have. You're not really going to find SD cards, definitely not anything like printed-out photos anymore. You have to go to Facebook. We're depending on servers somewhere in the ether to preserve all our evidence of ourselves.

The stakes of this archival dependence were both personal and high. Performers took for granted that their shows would be documented and shared, and they enjoyed having access to photos and videos of their drag lives, which helped them to evaluate old routines, brainstorm new ones, and promote upcoming events. Their comments about social media's imperfections stem not from the documentation and sharing of documenting their lives but rather from the near monopoly of the archiving. All of this documentation is gathered in a single vault—Facebook. Additional reservations concern Facebook policies that conflict with countercultural values, which I take up in the next section.

"Facebook Is Antidrag": Tensions of Online Realness

In the context of drag identity, no social media policy has been as controversial as Facebook's "real-name" rule. This policy has its roots in the platform's origins among elite universities. When Facebook was available only to students at Harvard, a school email address served as proof of affiliation and thus eligibility for an account. As Facebook expanded, it retained the policy of linking a user to an institutionally verified identity, citing commitments to safety. The refusal to accommodate pseudonyms has long been disputed by some privacy activists and Internet users, who point to early web history when pseudonyms were the norm (boyd 2012). In September 2014, tensions revolving around "real" names came to a head when Facebook froze over two hundred accounts belonging to drag queens. These users were told to use account names that corresponded to their legal identities, verified by state-issued identification documents, such as a driver's license. Given that Facebook was merely enforcing a longstanding policy, administrators did not expect the degree of outrage that ensued. An online petition from Change.org (Change.org 2014) gathered 45,000 signatures in a few weeks. Protests were held across the United States, with some of the most organized in San Francisco and Seattle. On October 2, 2014, Facebook issued a formal apology and announced the decision to overhaul the policy (Seals 2014; Tracer 2014).

In the wake of this controversy, Facebook instituted a number of policy tweaks. Its photo identification policies are triggered when text-based verification procedures are not possible. People who have names that correspond to conventionally accepted documentation can confirm their identity through one form of government identification or two forms of nongovernment documents. People who cannot verify their everyday names through either of those methods can submit two nongovernmental forms (such as mail or membership cards) and one additional identification (government-issued or not) that includes a photo or birthdate that matches the data entered on the Facebook account. The name on the third ID does not have to match the first two and is not added to the public Facebook account. The complex arrangements of documents at work in this agreement speak to the difficulty of pinning down a concept as multifaceted and elusive as a person's authentic identity. The adjusted policy reflects Facebook's expanded and more nuanced understanding of real names, demonstrated by the change in the policy from "real name" to "authentic name" in 2015.

In November 2015, I conducted an interview with Eva, a drag performer whose account was frozen in October for violating the authentic-name policy, a full year after Facebook promised to deal with this issue. In describing her experience, Eva addressed the stakes of having a Facebook account as well as the ways that individual identity is built into Facebook's design as a platform:

> Facebook is the way a lot of us promote events and talk to each other, recognize each other. [There are] a lot of people who identify through different identities, whether it's drag or the person is transgendered or just has a different identity for several other reasons and maybe doesn't have the resources to get those changes on their ID. It becomes a difficult place where you can't be who you want to be. You have to be who the government tells you to be. That's why I think it's really shitty. That's why I was kind of pissed. I feel kind of guilty because I didn't really think about it until it happened to me. At first, I was just, like, "Get over it. It's just a name." Then I was, like, "Oh, fuck." My thing is, I think it's hypocritical for Facebook to ask you what's on your mind but then censor you in such a way.

Eva's description covers a lot of ground—the need for drag performers to use Facebook, the different groups affected by Facebook's policy, and the paradox of identity censorship imposed by a platform that ostensibly is designed for expression. Given the amount of time, emotional labor, and artistic energy that Eva invested in Facebook, she responded to the account freeze with indignation and anger. Although Facebook purports to be a platform for self-expression, drag queens and others with fluid identities expose the ways in which only some expressions of identity are supported by Facebook's structure and policies.

As Eva noted, these kinds of policies matter for a number of groups besides drag queens, including transgender people who may not be out to their entire social networks (Haimson, Brubaker, et al. 2016); Native Americans and others who adopt multiple names to reflect their heritage (Phillip 2015); survivors of child abuse, sexual assault, and intimate partner violence; and police and journalist informants. All of these groups have a stake in the social media rules that surround names, and the capacity of online technologies to accommodate messy, fluid, or countercultural perceptions of identity. Yet one reason that Facebook's real-name policy gained so much traction among drag queens is that the word *real* is loaded in the context of drag. In ball culture, the word *realness* historically referred to the ability to perform a particular gender convincingly. Contemporary queer and feminist theory positions the rhetoric of realness as narrow-minded in conceptualizing gender and sexuality, particularly regarding trans people (Bailey 2011). Realness thus becomes part of a reductive, essentializing treatment of gender, and it was epitomized in Facebook's narrow concept of realness as something exclusively determined by a type of email address or official identification.

Many drag queens were aware of Facebook's real-name policy before the 2014 confrontation and had circulated tactics for how to get around it. As a participant in a 2013 focus group explained:

> Facebook is antidrag. It was made by the guys at Harvard who were meaning for college kids to hook up with each other. You didn't know how Facebook developed? You haven't seen *The Social Network*? When they opened [Facebook] up to the general public, it assumed that everyone has a first name and a last name. … I remember having to hack Facebook into letting me have one name. There was some tutorial where I had to trick my computer into thinking I was in Indonesia where they have one name. Then I had to change my language to Indonesian on Facebook. I have all the buttons memorized by the little Indonesian words. [Another queen] told me something changed, and she was, like, "The Facebook found me out." I was, like, "Oh, shit." I'm just a ticking time bomb waiting for them to demand a photocopy of my driver's license, which is the sixteen-year-old Christian kid from Alabama with braces and everything.

The central tension here was between users with complex relationships to identity and a platform that refused to accommodate those kinds of complexities. Presented with Facebook's strategies for organizing identity around first and last names, this participant developed tactics that resulted in considerable inconvenience (including claiming a false heritage and using an interface in a language that she could not read) as acceptable trade-offs for obtaining a user name that matched her stage name.

These comments also point to a design implication of how Facebook as a platform polices countercultural identity, an implication that touches on both legibility and authenticity. A key source of tension among the drag queens I interviewed is the lack of legibility in Facebook's mechanisms for policing membership. Accounts are frozen or locked through invisible processes of reporting. Without the ability to confront or even identify the users who flag profiles, drag queens voiced their own theories for explaining these decisions, often assigning them to larger narratives of homophobia and transphobia. When I asked one participant about why she thought that two of her friends had their accounts frozen in fall 2015, her response was immediate and damning: "Facebook is run by a bunch of homophobes." Although Facebook calls itself a community in the documents that explain its authentic-name policy, the lack of legibility in reporting keeps Facebook from feeling like a community to users who fall outside the scope of its dominant narratives of users.

Although the real-name policy provoked the most resentment among participants, as a whole Facebook was characterized as corporate, straight, and somewhat inflexible, even in design decisions that were less directly in opposition to drag identity. For example, Facebook's introduction of the Timeline (a feature that provides a stream of photos and updates and was introduced in 2011 and 2012) (Facebook 2016) required retroactive management of media, as discussed by participants in one focus group:

> Facebook changed, and now they have photos from when you were born. … I manage all my photos—like, all these photos that [showed up] when the new Facebook changed. Now no one can see my old photos.

> Remember when [another queen] posted a photo on Facebook—like, from when I did drag four years ago? [Laughter] Of course, my makeup wasn't fierce, and people were like, "Oh, my God!" and I was like, "Bitch, you better take that off."

Facebook's design decisions affect its entire user population, and many people besides drag queens felt inconvenienced or unnerved by the timeline as a platform intervention (Hamburger 2012). For example, the timeline feature is emotionally loaded for trans people who are trying to manage a diverse social network in which only some people might be aware of a user's transition (Haimson and Hoffman 2016). For drag queens and others who carefully manage their online media presence as part of the relational labor of maintaining social and professional relationships, the sudden emergence of uncurated photos into a highly curated stream of media was described as particularly disruptive.

As Sherri Grasmuck, Jason Martin, and Shanyang Zhao (2009, 164) note in their article on ethnoracial identity on Facebook, "the interface of Facebook makes some choices for users unavoidable while others are unavailable." In response to Facebook's "antidrag" interface with its alternately unavoidable and unavailable choices, drag queens developed various tactics of subversion and protest to cope with and contest what participants perceived as the platform's demands for simple, heteronormative expressions of identity.

Conclusions

As recently as February 2016, drag queens in my network were still having their accounts frozen, although a December 2015 policy change was intended to resolve this issue for once and for all. In addition to the expanded identification options outlined earlier in this chapter, the new policy on accepted IDs includes mail addressed to a user's preferred name and information from users' social feeds (Holpuch 2015). For example, a search through a user's messages that shows multiple friends addressing the user by her preferred name becomes a form of name verification. The new policy also asks those who report name violations to describe how the user being reported is violating a policy, which could potentially decrease the number of complaints motivated out of homophobia or transphobia. Although these revisions are an important step, they still do not address a practice that was common among the queens I interviewed, which is maintaining both a queen account and a boy account. Currently, Facebook still insists that users maintain only one account.

Yet even if Facebook's newest policy tweaks address its most divisive design problems, the controversy over "authentic" identity is revealing in the context of countercultural identity and digital media platforms. Facebook does not allow users flexibility in reshaping the platform's interface. However odd someone's interests are or unusual someone's name is, these differences are flattened out into homogeneous metadata fields that are identical in structure, if not in content. Within the rigid structure of Facebook's profile template, drag queens developed their own tactics of flexibility, evidenced in practices of maintaining multiple accounts (boy and queen, everyday and performer) and tricking the platform into thinking that a user was from a country like Indonesia to avoid rules about surnames. My arguments that online platforms should offer sociotechnical flexibility to support countercultural communities should not suggest that ad hoc tactics are not possible on mainstream platforms like Facebook. My point is that whereas a countercultural platform would see this kind of flexibility as a design value to be fostered, corporate platforms like Facebook see these tactics as a violation of community standards.

In addition to Facebook's tendency toward inflexibility, its user policies also lack legibility. As Kate Crawford and Tarleton Gillespie (2014) argue in their review of flagging policies across social media sites, platforms often offer flags so that users can monitor each other's behavior according to a set of rules, typically the terms of service or user guidelines. Yet individuals who attempt to contest Facebook's policies encounter an infrastructure that is meant to be navigated rather than critiqued. The drag queens I interviewed regarded Facebook's real-name/authentic-name policy as homophobic and prejudiced, which suggests that there is a need for a legible process that allows people who flag and are flagged to understand the procedures shaping their engagement with the site and other users. A meaningful commitment to legibility would require the adjudication process to be more than nominally participatory, in the sense that users can participate by flagging content that they see as inappropriate or offensive. To better accommodate complex, messy and queer identities, the process needs to be legible, meaning that users can easily trace and contest the reporting structure for alleged violations of Facebook's policies.

Given these constraints on flexibility and legibility from the viewpoint of countercultural communities, how can mainstream social media sites be made to fit local needs? Within the scope of legibility, flexibility, and authenticity, Facebook's change of the name of its naming policy from real-name to authentic-name is (unintentionally, of course) fitting. Although Facebook's definition of authenticity is clearly different from mine, we both agree that as people continue to use online technologies in their everyday lives, authenticity is at once desirable, valuable, and problematic.

People use online platforms for a wide range of social functions, including professional and educational needs, dating, parenting, hobbies, religion, and ethically questionable activities like fraud and theft. Not all of these goals are well-suited to Facebook's value of authenticity, which links online identity work to a rigid, mainstream notion of self and individuality. After analyzing public comments from Facebook's Mark Zuckerberg on the topic of anonymity, authenticity, and identity, Oliver Haimson and Anna Lauren Hoffmann (2016, sec. "The Disconnect between Discourse, Design, and Authentic Presentation," para. 3) concluded:

> If we accept authenticity and identity as something that is constructed or performed in context, and if some constructions or performances cannot be reconciled with Facebook's "real name" policies, then we begin to see the ways that Facebook simultaneously demands and forestalls authentic presentation.

I have described authenticity as the capacity of online technologies to accommodate local values and ethics or the ability of platforms to allow users to see themselves in the technologies that they use. In closing this chapter, I consider the concept of authenticity in terms of how the drag queens I interviewed navigated the perceived straightness of Facebook and what it means for digital technologies to support countercultural forms of belonging by allowing them to misfit rather than fit neatly within a platform.

After the 2014 policy debate, many people asked why Facebook should appease drag queens. After all, if they don't like Facebook's policies, they don't have to use its service. But this argument fails to appreciate the amount of labor that users put into maintaining their Facebook accounts, the content they post and curate, the conversations they have, and the connections they form—all of which provide the data that Facebook monetizes in its advertising. Telling users that they can simply go elsewhere if they don't like the rules dismisses the extent to which they need to be viewed as stakeholders in the sites that depend on user-generated content (Brunton and Nissenbaum 2015). In addition, although no platform can be all things to all people, when people who are disproportionately affected by a given policy are the same people who have been historically disenfranchised and marginalized, a platform needs to ask whether its policies are not only exclusionary but discriminatory.

Although they were not the first to protest Facebook's real-name policy, drag queens made headway with Facebook where others did not for two key reasons: they embraced their lack of fit within the system, and they acted collectively. One important factor to their success was that rather than looking for ways to make their queerness fit into a straight interface, drag queens drew on a range of practices that celebrated their alterity. Rosemarie Garland-Thomson's (2011, 592–593) work on the concept of the misfit is useful here:

> *fitting* and *misfitting* denote an encounter in which two things come together in either harmony or disjunction. When the shape and substance of these two things correspond in their union, they fit. A *misfit*, conversely, describes an incongruent relationship between two things: a square peg in a round hole. The problem with a misfit, then, inheres not in either of the two things but rather in their juxtaposition, the awkward attempt to fit them together. … Misfits are inherently unstable rather than fixed, yet they are very real because they are material rather than linguistic constructions. The discrepancy between body and world, between that which is expected and that which is, produces fits and misfits.

Although Garland-Thomson does not use the concept of misfitting to consider issues of values in design, her work is instructive in the context of drag queens and social media. The core components of misfits—their instability, their materiality, and their emergence from the actual rather than the expected—can be applied to how drag queens perceived their relationships to Facebook as a mainstream, sociotechnical platform.

Participants' tactics for using Facebook reflect an attempt to manage this "discrepancy between body and world, between that which is expected and that which is." Initially, these tactics concentrated on workarounds and hacks, such as listing oneself as Indonesian to circumvent the first-name/last-name requirement. When accounts were frozen, the stakes of misfitting grew higher, and instead of fitting themselves into a platform that they perceived as too strict (and too straight), drag queens fought for ways to retain their status as misfits, insisting on their authenticity within Facebook as a platform. Authenticity—the ability of users to see themselves in the policies and design of a site that they use every day—moved to the center of the debate.

A second important factor in their success was that drag queens are typically comfortable with visibility in ways that other groups affected by the real-name policy—survivors of sexual assault and child abuse, for example—might not be. The very source of stigma that makes drag queens a target for the flagging of their accounts lends itself to an aptitude for raising awareness and garnering attention. In addition to this embrace of a sociotechnical misfit, drag queens were able to effect change because they acted collectively rather than individually. Drag queens led an initiative to demand changes to Facebook's policies, which would not have been possible if the initiative had been undertaken by an individual misfit; a community of misfits was required.

Remembering the preferred terms among participants in this study, Brooklyn drag queens overwhelmingly described themselves as a community and as nested within larger queer, artistic, and urban communities. The layering of networks emerged as an organizing tactic for drag queens who wanted to protest Facebook's policy. In addition to working within their own community to demand action, they built coalitions with other groups whose identities were misfits with Facebook's identity policy. Drag queens' willingness to build external alliances demonstrates the efficacy of acting collectively and was a key factor in their successful call for platform policies that could better accommodate misfits.

Given the effect that community action can have in forcing a policy change, I want to close by considering what *community* means in a conventional Facebook context versus a countercultural context. When Facebook calls itself a community, it refers to its goal of creating a hospitable framework for its many users.[5] For example, its "Community Standards" document (Facebook 2016) states that "the conversations that happen on Facebook reflect the diversity of a community of more than one billion people" and that "our global community is growing every day and we strive to welcome people to an environment free from abusive content."

On the surface level, we might consider to what extent any group with one billion people could be considered a community. Is China a community? The global south? When is it useful to think of Christians as a community? Republicans? Marxist feminists? But even setting aside the question of whether and how a community scales, there are questions of what kinds of community are imagined as belonging to the Facebook community. People under age thirteen are not welcome in Facebook's community, for instance, nor are people who seek to produce a sense of social connectivity by circulating sexually explicit images. And until recently, people whose account names did not match their state-issued ID did not belong either.

Rather than trying to carve out a coherent sense of community in its standards, Facebook's concept of community is vague and loosely articulated in instructions for how to report abusive behavior and protect users' intellectual property. In this sense, Facebook's stance toward community is similar to what writers like Miranda Joseph (2002) have critiqued in the use of the term in the social sciences. For Joseph, the word *community* has become an empty signifier laden with valences of anticapitalism and social equality and uncontested in its status as an unequivocally good thing. But communities are typically rife with the same power structures that underlie capitalism and often lack social equality. In fact, communities are not always good things, either for their constituents (such as cults that involve nonconsensual sex) or within larger social spheres (such as domestic terrorist groups).

Countercultural groups cannot afford to adopt a similarly rosy or vague view of what it means to belong to their community, online or offline, if they want to survive. This is why IAM's terms of service were integral for its users and why New Brunswick punks were sometimes critical of but ultimately stood by the sociotechnical practices that simultaneously protected them from the police and created exclusionary politics. Like Brooklyn drag queens, these groups see themselves as a forming community because they share specific ethics and norms, which manifest in their treatment of digital technologies.

I am not suggesting that Facebook be demonized as soulless and capitalist or as opposed to alterity (generally) or drag queens (specifically). Throughout this chapter, I document the ways in which participants enjoyed and benefitted from using Facebook in their lives as performers and queer people. I see a shared practice-based understanding in both Facebook's and Brooklyn drag queens' approaches to community. Recall that participants defined themselves as belonging to a local community partly because of how they performed drag, a definition based on what they *do* rather than *who they are*. Similarly, in its community guidelines, Facebook offers a list of do's and don'ts for reporting behavior and policies on abusive language, which also can be viewed as a practice-based approach to defining community. The fundamental difference here is in tying these practices to a local set of values and norms, which I have labeled as authenticity.

Whereas Facebook conceptualizes community as the lowest common denominator of shared online interaction, drag queens think of community as a set of commitments to gender, sexuality, on-stage aesthetics, and alterity. They see their community as one of misfits, and moreover as a community of misfits to be celebrated from the outset, even while filling out the data fields of a profile. Instead of viewing community as something that happens within the site itself, countercultural communities see the politics of online platforms at the design level. Many aspects of a site—the profile metadata, the terms of service, the display of social networks, and the policies for verifying identity—can either support or exclude countercultural identities, allowing members to fit in or be misfits. The gaps between supporting and excluding point to the capacity of digital technologies to provide a sense of belonging to communities of alterity.

6 Countercultural Values for Theory and in Design

This book tells the stories of people who have been brought together and driven apart by digital technology. Drawing on years of qualitative fieldwork, I have sketched the different practices and tactics that take shape as these groups work to build, sustain, and protect their collective sense of identity and alterity. Countercultural narratives complicate, disrupt, and reorient conventional assumptions about the role that technology plays in daily digital life, providing a richer, more complex narrative of digital media. I have highlighted the ethics of legibility, flexibility, and authenticity as a way of identifying how tensions between mainstream and outsider narratives of digital technologies are operationalized and how broader discourses about technology manifest in everyday tactics and practices.

My first field study looked at *Body Modification Ezine* (BME), which grew out of an early and experimental phase of online community building and came into its own as the now-dominant social media platforms were beginning to sprout. BME delivered on some of the earliest promises of online technologies—connecting people across distances, convening a public of misfits who would otherwise have struggled to find opportunities for regular interaction, and allowing its users to engage in conversation and reveal parts of themselves in ways that many felt were impossible in offline contexts. In analyzing some of the changes made to IAM's terms of service (TOS) throughout the site's history, I identified different experiments in managing membership. BME's policies were not perfect. Rules could be unevenly or subjectively enforced by administrators. Nonetheless, these processes offered a high degree of legibility, as shown in users' ability to trace rules and policies in the site's day-to-day operations. IAM elevated the TOS from a routine, default document to an evolving, commonly referenced set of guidelines that were subject to community feedback and incorporated into daily interactions, conversations, and disputes. IAM's reliance on an open structure of feedback on its policies (and their enforcement) contrasts with illegible platforms that make rules of use and membership obscure to ordinary users. A key point here is that legibility is not just something technical: it is also fundamentally social. IAM's TOS is significant not because of its technical features but because it became so ingrained in the social conversations and understandings of membership.

Ultimately, however, external rather than internal forces were most responsible for IAM's decline. In terms of both media content and user participation, IAM was eventually replaced by Facebook. This transition took shape not through a hostile, corporate takeover but through the mass defection of members who were lured by larger audiences and more sophisticated design features. The site struggled to convince its members to continue posting on IAM rather than competing, mainstream venues, and eventually body modification user groups sprung up on Facebook, exporting content directly from BME. As a field study, BME and IAM point to a key de Certeauian tension of cultural politics—the struggle to retain a sense of identity and alterity amid hegemonic cultural institutions.

Communities of alterity develop sociotechnical practices in ways that respond to and reflect their relationships to the mainstream, playing out across many different sociotechnical relationships. For members of New Brunswick's punk community, part of the allure in using older, less sophisticated technologies has to do with positioning themselves as countercultural. For example, their limited engagement with Facebook (at least in the context of show information) is intended to demonstrate a commitment to DIY and punk values. The basement community represents itself as being on the margins through aesthetic choices (in how they dress and what kind of music they play) and through their relationships to technology. In contrast to dominant narratives that young people are dependent on Facebook for their communication needs, New Brunswick punks take a critical and measured approach to mainstream social network sites. In addition, they have also embraced older platforms, such as message boards and paper flyers as familiar forms of media and communication. In the basement community, representations of alterity take shape in the different technological assemblages that inform how fans find out about a show's location and in the flexible gatekeeping mechanisms that reflect commitments to secrecy.

There are many reasons to leverage online technologies in the service of secrecy, such as criminal behavior (Brunton 2013) and political resistance to surveillance (Bossewitch and Sinnreich 2012). The defining features of the New Brunswick basement community's relationships to technology are flexibility and authenticity, where a sense of collective commitment and solidarity draw on local understandings of DIY values. Practices of secrecy among New Brunswick basement members make for an interesting contrast with a site like Silk Road, an online clearinghouse for quasi-legal and illegal assets like drugs and store coupons. Both are invested in keeping secrets from the police, but the sociotechnical practices in the former are concerned with collectivity, ideology, and values, whereas the latter's are a fairly straightforward attempt to keep legally perilous activities undercover. In other words, Silk Road users are interested in keeping their own activities private, where New Brunswick punks are interested in keeping their community events secret in a commitment to localized, DIY values. Even members of the basement community who felt that the rules of communication might be overly constraining or performative ultimately expressed a willingness to comply because not doing so risked ostracism from the community. In the New Brunswick basement community, individual technologies and platforms come and go, and sociotechnical flexibility is key to the community's longevity.

For Brooklyn's drag community, the focus of my final field study, mainstream social media sites like Facebook and Instagram are vital tools on both individual and community levels. Platforms like Instagram supported the promotional work of advertising upcoming shows and provided a digital record of performances. Social media sites provided an important archive of the trajectory of performances, which participants described as important for personal development and for the relational labor of maintaining their fan base (Baym 2015). Many drag queens were self-taught seamstresses and makeup artists, and they described using YouTube videos and Instagram photos to hone their skills of getting "in face." Digital technologies were also vital in forging and maintaining community ties, both on the local level of connecting to other drag queens who lived nearby and also on the level of connecting Brooklyn drag to a larger archive and community of queer culture. Yet even as mainstream social media fill these important roles, the performers I interviewed were conflicted about the consequences of using these sites to archive, connect, and communicate. They were wary of (and fatigued by) a pervasive sense of relying on social media platforms and worried about the long-term social consequences of technological dependence, such as alienating or antisocial behavior.

More specific to their identities as drag performers, participants were frustrated by policies that they experienced as illegible, inflexible, and anti-queer. Several participants viewed Facebook as a homophobic platform, and they experienced Facebook's policies on authentic names as problematic for their identities as drag queens. The real-name/authentic-name policy was even more troubling in terms of the opacity of reporting users for violations. When queens had their pages frozen, they had no way to create a dialogue between users who reported each other or between users and Facebook administrators. Participants found it frustrating that Facebook claimed to want its users to express themselves and document their lives only to censor those expressions through policies that demand normative identities. This tension is one of authenticity, which I have presented as the ability of members of a countercultural community to see its values and norms reflected in the platforms that they use in their everyday lives.

I now want to return to a core question woven throughout the field studies comprising this book: how do online technologies help or hinder community building? The answers matter for sociologists, tech designers, activists, policy makers, and individual web users. Given these different stakeholders, I unpack two sets of implications—the first for Internet studies scholarship and the second for design. First, I concentrate on the extension of my analytical framework and methodological approach. I advocate for the kinds of projects and methods that can further develop an accounting of technological alterity in the context of digital technologies. Second, I consider implications for design. Drawing on the framework of flexibility, legibility, and authenticity, what implications are there for building better online platforms? What policies, governance guidelines, and design ethics can we tease out to support communities of alternative people?

Implications for Theory

The practices and tactics that countercultural communities develop are part of a process of making different technologies meet their needs and sometimes even feel like home. Countercultural practices stem from a gap between fitting and misfitting in a sociotechnical system, and it is from this gap that I can speak back to some longstanding debates in Internet and media studies theory. These debates are introduced in chapter 2 as the strategic narratives against and within which countercultural tactics operate. Looking across the communities that I have studied, I concentrate on dynamics of space, anonymity, and media activism.

Trade-offs in Mobility and Place

Part of what countercultural communities do online is to make the platforms and systems that they use feel like home, meaning a shared sense of place. In chapter 2, I warn against spatial metaphors for the Internet, so I want to avoid similarly careless comparisons between the web and space here. However, my objections to spatial metaphors are rooted in a need to be attentive to the metaphors and euphemisms that surround a particular technology. Spatial metaphors for the Internet are paradoxically invested in presenting space as immaterial and inconsequential. These assumptions are particularly apparent in a "mobile first" design ethic, which assumes that mobile phones rather than desktop computers should be the primary design case for online platforms. The emphasis on apps and cross-platforms has been known to leave out those who are disconnected or minimally connected (Crawford 2013), but in addition, we need to ask about those who prefer to produce their own sense of place through online interactions. What about communities that value online platforms because they provide a sense of copresence?

When I asked Rachel Larratt, the current owner of BME, about the claims in Facebook's user guidelines (Facebook 2015) that it is a "global community," she rejected this bid for shared togetherness: "It's all marketing … they are trying to foster that idea [of being a community]. It's just staged, really, like a big box store trying to pretend like they are a local small business owner." Herself a small business owner, Rachel does not reject the commercial interests of Facebook, just its claim that Facebook as a whole constitutes a community. Later in the interview, Rachel returned to this metaphor of Facebook as a giant chain store:

> Facebook is the Walmart of the Internet. Facebook came to town and just put out of business all of these smaller niche sites. … People are starting to revolt, to be like, "No, we don't want a Walmart in our town." Or they try and rebuild their

> downtown areas where they have all these very cool old buildings that have all been abandoned ... because nobody can compete with products that are of lower quality [but] for a lower price. It's just more of the optimist in me that I'm hoping it'll come back.

Regardless of the future of BME, Rachel hopes that a certain kind of Internet culture—with features that I call authentic, in that they reflect local values and ethics—will cycle back into favor.

Two implications about mobility and place can be made from Rachel's comments. One has to do with retaining a sense of localized and countercultural authenticity, which I address in the next section. Another, somewhat subtler dimension of these metaphors has to do with how digital technologies are imagined as overcoming barriers of space. Rachel's metaphors of gentrification and urban renewal reflect the de Certeauian element of making do and poaching within existing sociocultural structures, and her optimism imagines a collective uprising against the conformity of mainstream social media. Rachel identifies a kind of placelessness as the unavoidable consequence of a massive user base, much as the generic predictability of Walmart contrasts with the authentic idiosyncrasies of locally owned retail and grocery stores. This dominance of the generic over the authentic and of the mass market over the localized reveals a connection to a design ethic that privileges mobility over stability. Assuming that mobility and constant connectivity are a paradigm of access comes at the expense of recognizing the importance for online communities in feeling grounded, of feeling that their online platforms give them a sustained sense of place and copresence. Designing platforms that are geared toward mobile devices and interoperability reflects assumptions that convenience is more important than other features of online interaction, such as a sustained, grounded sense of place.

The contemporary push toward mobility assumes that people want a sense of seamless fluidity as they engage with different online platforms from their mobile devices, reflecting a "going with" rather than "going to" approach of online access. But for those who value the sense of feeling as if they are visiting a physical meeting point, seamlessness can be experienced as a loss rather than a feature. This is not an antiprogress push for a return to less sophisticated technologies but rather a call to consider whether mobility is ubiquitously desirable and who is best served by a push for the sense of uninterrupted access. Perhaps countercultural communities should pause before embracing mobility as a design goal because it is more conducive to community cohesion to think of going online as going to a space. In her work on for-profit educational institutions, Tressie McMillan Cottom (2014) has argued persuasively that much of the rhetoric of online education positions students as "roaming auto-didacts," people whose work and family commitments are endlessly flexible and who have the necessary tools for minimal interpersonal contact with professors and other students. "Mobile first" rhetoric contains similar assumptions about mobility and place*less*ness, which can be deeply problematic for communities that seek a sense of place*full*ness.

Pseudonyms, Anonyms, Multinyms

Powerful actors in the tech community have all but dismissed the possibility of using social media anonymously. In 1999, Sun Microsystems' chief executive, Scott McNealy, said, "You have zero privacy anyway. Get over it." In a 2009 CNBC interview, Eric Schmidt of Google said of online behavior, "If you have something that you don't want anyone to know, maybe you shouldn't be doing it in the first place." In 2010, Mark Zuckerberg of Facebook argued that privacy was "no longer a social norm" (all quotes cited in Popkin 2011). In the "nym wars" that oppose these views, advocates have argued for experimentation and play, and detractors have argued that crime, fraud, and harassment flourish when people do not have to use their real names. Tensions between social media policies and identity work surface in chapter 5, with drag queens squaring off against Facebook about how to verify accounts. Multinyms might be a better way of thinking about the relationships that Brooklyn drag performers have to names and identity, as they passionately defend the right to post self-determined (rather than state-determined) names on social media and to maintain multiple accounts on the same platform. Complexities of verifying identity also mattered for New Brunswick punks who were determining which request for information about music show locations should be honored and which should be deemed fraudulent. Another practice of secrecy and naming surfaced in the use of codenames for show houses, intended to cloak basement venues from those outside the punk information loop. Practices from both communities point to the importance of thinking about pseudonyms and anonyms as a form of ethical identity work.

Not all social media sites insist on state-verified identity. Some are anonymous (such as YikYak, Whisper, and the now-defunct Secret), and others encourage pseudonyms or throwaway handles (like Reddit and 4chan). These latter sites tend to be associated with harassment and crude conversations (although online harassment also commonly occurs on Facebook, Twitter, and YouTube). Although it is common to conflate pseudonyms with illicit behavior—despite some research indicating that anonymity encourages pro-social interactions, with communication norms more in keeping with older Internet technologies like Internet Relay Chats (IRCs) and message boards (Ma, Hancock, and Naaman 2016)—the association between pseudonyms, anonyms, and criminal behavior is not innate but is developed over time. Criminals use pseudonyms, and anonymity can lead people to act inappropriately, but positive outcomes also result from platforms that are flexible enough to help sustain identity work. The data that I have gathered provide grounded accounts of when pseudonymity fosters rather than threatens community. Facebook's real-name/authentic-name controversy uncovered reasons that someone might have for using names other than the one assigned at birth. New Brunswick punks demonstrated how secrecy can be part of what preserves local culture and respects local community.

An increasingly common component of login interfaces involves cross-account linking, also called *bootstrapping*, which makes issues of identity work and data privacy even more complex. Bootstrap logins require or encourage users first to log into or have an account with another platform, like the way that the dating app Tindr requires people to have an account on Facebook. Typically sold to users as a form of convenience, bootstrapping has important consequences for data and privacy. Cross-platform logins create tangles of identifying information that make it difficult for users to retain a sense of control over their own data or a sense of experimentation and play with identity. Internet studies research needs to move beyond studying single platforms and begin to investigate cross-platform behaviors. How do users trace the flows of their data across multiple platforms? What tactics do people use to retain a sense of selfhood and individuality? With sites becoming more integrated via mechanisms like bootstrapping, we need scholarship that is similarly mobile in accounting for data and identity.

Countercultural Social Movements

As a way of bridging implications for theory and practice, I want to draw connections between the tactics of countercultural communities and activist groups. Even activists who do not focus on the Internet as an issue often use tools and devices that reflect social justice values, such as using open-source code or products made by companies that incorporate fair labor practices. Like the New Brunswick punks who were willing to accept some inconveniences in information flows to avoid unwanted attention from the authorities, activist groups may opt for less sophisticated or user-friendly communication tools to demonstrate solidarity with other activists or laborers. Yet decisions around using open-source platforms, for example, may not be as straightforward as they at first seem.

For example, Veronica Barassi (2015) has unpacked some of the ways that efforts to identify parallels in technology use and ideology can be cumbersome or work at cross-purposes with goals of inclusion and access. Recalling how Brooklyn drag queens described Facebook, people can simultaneously enjoy features of a mainstream platform and also have serious reservations about using it. Activist groups may insist on using open-source technologies or avoid buying products that are made in inhumane working conditions, but this is only one kind of ethical orientation to digital technologies. For some groups, it may be as important to ask how a technology will be used as it is to ask how it is produced.

Media activism is a growing area of study that offers important accounts of how power is contested and distributed online. We need more research on how people manage ideological conflicts with the platforms they use, and looking at activist groups is a smart way to do this. Yet much of current social movement research in Internet studies has concentrated on leftist and progressive movements (Costanza-Chock 2014; Pickard 2006; Wolfson 2014). Focusing on conservative and ultraconservative activist groups could yield important insights into how people make sense of platform politics. I see value in studying marginalized and countercultural communities because it expands our understanding of how and by whom the Internet is used. It is equally important to be expansive in the social movements that are studied in research on digital technologies and activism.

Countercultural Values in Design

Throughout this text, I have developed a framework of legibility, flexibility, and authenticity for evaluating the capacities of different online platforms, tools, and practices to support countercultural communities. Similar to Sarah Pink's (2014) approach to design anthropology, this framework is both conceptual and pragmatic, and provides a way of thinking about sociotechnical assemblages for supporting community and alterity. In the remainder of this chapter, I consider implications for how online tools can support projects of community, particularly for members of countercultural groups who might not be able to locate each other without online platforms or might have ideological qualms with the wholesale adoption of mainstream sites like Facebook and Twitter.

Offering pragmatic suggestions for evaluating and reworking digital technologies makes theory less abstract and grounds analysis in the daily uses, operations, and policies of a platform. These design values are not a checklist but are a set of lenses for encouraging multiple levels of thoughtfulness about the intended audiences for a given platform. My hope is that this framework can be adapted for analyzing other online platforms in the context of community (see figure 6.1). Straddling contributions for theory as well as design and drawing from all three field studies, the following

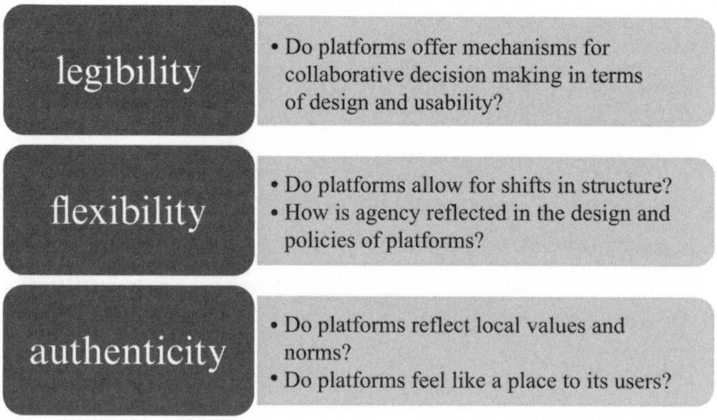

Figure 6.1
In this table, design value questions are associated with the three-part analytical framework that structures this book (legibility, flexibility, and authenticity). The design values are intended as provocations rather than a strict checklist.

sections describe the different means that countercultural groups have developed to build and sustain community.

Middle Ground on Mainstream Platforms

There are two main avenues for design in the context of technology, alterity, and community—design that develops stand-alone countercultural technologies and design that works within mainstream platforms to make them more legible, flexible, and authentic. The field studies that are examined in this book offer different approaches to both work within and reject mainstream social media sites. BME grew out of its own distinctive community platform, which originally was coded and maintained by community members. In contrast, drag queens used Facebook rather than develop their own platform, although participants described ethical reservations and tactical workarounds that made the platform meet their needs. New Brunswick punks fell somewhere in between, using Facebook and Twitter up to a point while also maintaining older, more alternative platforms like message boards. Between developing countercultural platforms and operating within those that already exist, the New Brunswick punk community fashioned a kind of middle position.

This is in some sense puzzling; given the New Brunswick punk community's commitment to older technologies, one might ask why it engaged with Facebook at all. Flyers and text messages anchored communication among a core group of dedicated members, making it reasonable to avoid other forms of technology. In interviews, participants frequently expressed a kind of grim resignation to using Facebook to communicate with others in the basement community. They saw their use of Facebook as pragmatic because bands and their audiences consist largely of young adults who increasingly prefer to communicate through social media platforms, particularly over other communication tools like email (Philipson 2014). Because most bands both consist of and have audiences who are young adults, platforms like Facebook (and to a lesser degree, Myspace) are all but required means of organizing tours.

Another factor that supports a tool like Facebook is the turnover in the community. With the local university providing a constant flow of students into the city, New Brunswick punks are to some extent beholden to whatever communication technologies dominate in the pool of potential community members. This pragmatic approach to using mainstream platforms within a countercultural context has a parallel with drag queens who promote themselves on Facebook to gain wide audiences, despite reservations about the platform as homophobic and antidrag. Both examples illustrate tactical maneuvering with even the most mainstream technologies. The New Brunswick punk community viewed Facebook as one part of a sociotechnical assemblage and assigned different roles to different platforms. For example, Facebook helped people learn that a show was happening, texting helped them get there, and message boards were used to talk about shows and bands. Brooklyn drag queens developed a number of hacks and workarounds to make Facebook suit their needs, carving out their own sociotechnical affordances for authenticity when the platform presented none. In their willingness to use mainstream platforms while developing workarounds to mitigate the limitations of those platforms, communities of alterity can build relationships to technology that reflect countercultural authenticity, even if those platforms are otherwise geared both implicitly and explicitly toward the mainstream.

Mainstream Creep

Mainstream creep, a concept that I mention briefly in chapter 3, is another manifestation of the mainstream's potentially damaging influence on the online presence of countercultural communities. At some point, every online platform faces the question of whether and how to redesign. As new programming languages emerge, typically bringing more powerful and sophisticated technical capabilities, social media administrators often worry that unless their site keeps up, users will leave for newer sites with more appealing design aesthetics. And yet redesigning a site to keep up with technological advances can have unintended consequences, as was the case for IAM. Competition from mainstream social media sites led BME's owners to redesign the platform. For the first time, non-BME members coded the site's interface, and more important, mainstream social media aesthetics started to appear in IAM's design. The site lost some of its sense of countercultural authenticity, and some longtime users began to question the countercultural values of BME's leadership.

In contrast, the field study of the New Brunswick punk scene demonstrates the potential advantages (from a countercultural perspective) of embracing older platforms and technologies as part of a commitment to DIY values and ethics. During fieldwork, I repeatedly found that countercultural communities place less value on having the latest technologies and more on being able to trace, influence, and control structures of power and to represent themselves online in ways that reflect their local values. In this way, resisting the lure of updates can be an important means of retaining authenticity by reflecting the history of a community and its changing relationships to a particular site. Such reflections are about the materials that are produced and circulated online and also are about process. Both the content itself and the ways that it got online must represent the countercultural identity. For communities of alterity, the means for building a platform can matter just as much as the ends. Perhaps users enjoy the stability precisely because many other sites are malleable. Or perhaps the simpler, less sophisticated features act as a sorting mechanism that weeds out users in a way that supports a sense of closeness. Either way, the success of New Brunswick's message boards (as well as sites like Craigslist and Reddit) and the difficulties encountered by BME suggest that communities might endure not in spite of a refusal to upgrade but because of it.

The Permanent Sandbox

All three of the countercultural design values that I identify (legibility, flexibility, and authenticity) are bound up in the principle of the permanent sandbox, by which I mean giving users mechanisms for altering or adding platform operations. In software design, the word *sandbox* typically refers to a prerelease version of an application where the client or end user can experiment with features and make suggestions for improvement. Instead of thinking of the sandbox as an early, finite development period, designers could build in mechanisms for user feedback into the long-term operation of the platform. I should be clear that integrating this type of configurability is distinct from redesigning for the sake of redesigning. The latter contributes to a cycle of perpetual techno-obsolescence in which devices are replaced not because they break or become unusable but because they are seen to need improvement for aesthetic or status-based reasons (Gehl 2014), with serious environmental consequences. Instead, I am suggesting a design ethic that incorporates respect for flexibility, granting users sufficient agency to guide the design of the platforms that they themselves sustain.

This shift toward user feedback and influence also could occur through a return to the flexibility of sites like Myspace. The (user-determined) messiness of profiles was commonly considered a design flaw of Myspace, both implicitly and explicitly supporting claims that the site was unsafe and a playground for predators (Marwick 2008). Yet in its place, we now have the incomprehensibility of Facebook's shifting advertising sidebar and news feed, which are not in the user's direct control (Couldry and Turow 2014; Eslami et al. 2015; Turow 2011). As a kaleidoscope of fonts, colors, and sounds, Myspace reflected user agency and individuality. Facebook is similarly in flux as a platform with constantly updated content, but its aesthetic and structural malleability is less visible to everyday users. When users object to a sudden design change or new usability feature, the problem is not necessarily the updated feature but often is the lack of legibility that preceded its arrival. I would argue that users can be trusted to adjust to an aesthetic that is more complex and less structured than Facebook or Twitter currently offers, especially when they have a degree of agency in these changes.

Return to the TOS

Most Internet users have adopted a blasé attitude toward corporate end-user license agreements (EULAs), sometimes also called clickwrap. Because corporations rely on clickwrap to protect themselves from the misuse of their software, average Internet users would have to spend 250 hours a year reading all of the legal documents presented to them as they go about their everyday online lives (Masnick 2012). EULAs are a tricky form of displayed obscurity—Although clickwrap documents provide detailed rules for using software or participating in a platform, their wording is so inaccessible for most web users as to be all but unintelligible. As a different model for informing users of their rights and responsibilities, I suggest a return to the terms of service (TOS). IAM treated its user guidelines as a document that mattered in everyday online life. This approach to the TOS involves thinking of user guidelines not as corporate legal agreements but as living documents that account for local constituents' values and practices.

On the most rudimentary level, Internet policy and legal scholars have found that when terms of service and end-user license agreements are presented in common speech or include a bullet point list of key issues, users are more likely to read and understand these texts (Newitz 2005). More radically, I see the fluidity of IAM's TOS and its emphasis on participation and feedback as an argument for a more collaborative crafting of a platform's policies. Building a document through community input and consensus is difficult, as has been demonstrated in general assemblies at Occupy Wall Street (Occupy Wall Street 2013) and in Iceland's attempts to crowdsource its constitution (Landemore 2014). Yet in a truly participatory process of collective sense making, the *process* of inclusion is as important as the *product* of guidelines and policies. Numerous platforms (including wikis and github) already exist for collectively designing a document. Rather than an artifact that is written by corporate lawyers with an eye toward legal culpability, a community TOS could be produced as a wiki that includes legible mechanisms for feedback and adjudication. If an online platform is truly committed to supporting community, then its users should be able to shape and contest (and not just access) its policies.

Intersectional Design Ethics

When designers try to accommodate particular communities in the structures and features of an online platform, they often design for one dimension of a user to the exclusion of other dimensions. Rather than thinking of personas (or an imagined set of specific user profiles to use for feature development) (Miaskiewicz and Kozar 2011), designers could think in terms of communities. This approach could be called *intersectional design ethics*—a set of values that considers the multifaceted nature of community identity.

Any design process that privileges communities over individuals needs to remember crossover and multiple memberships. In the introduction to this book, I describe three different types of community—based on practice, geography, and alterity—noting that although these categories are distinct, they often overlap. For example, New Brunswick's basement punk community has developed a set of tactics for managing information that are rooted in its sense of alterity and commitment to the countercultural ethics of DIY production. But these tactics are also shaped by geography, in that the city is both a college town and a key stopping point between New York and Philadelphia. Concentrating exclusively on either alterity or geography tells only part of the story of how this community uses technology.

Conclusions: Communities of Alterity and/as Communities of Play

Julie Cohen (2012) has argued that the design of online technologies in support of play and creativity is a matter of human flourishing. It follows that developing tools for creativity and play is also a matter of community flourishing. Considering the different avenues for design and practice is relevant not just to people who belong to countercultural communities but also to a much wider set of stakeholders. Values-in-design conversations can have crucial legal and financial implications, in that heading off potential lawsuits or user protests can save time, money, and reputation. In the tech industry, concerns over privacy and ethics are provoked in part by high-profile cases of academic and industry researchers who overstep their authority or ignore longstanding norms of human subject research (Schroeder 2014). In suggesting the above design interventions, my goal has been to show how legibility, flexibility, and authenticity are not just part of a theoretical framework but also part of a discussion about how to build digital technologies in ways that support community flourishing.

The tactics and assemblages produced by the three groups that are examined in this book reflect the affordances and obstacles that technology provides for building and sustaining community. A close look at communities of alterity offers a vantage point for identifying the gaps between design and use, the strategic and the tactical, the mainstream and the misfit. Rosemarie Garland-Thomson (2011, 592) argues that "misfitting as an explanatory concept lets us think through a particular aspect of world-making involved in material-discursive becoming." As these groups of misfits incorporate digital technologies into the everyday tasks and interactions of community life, they bring into relief the embedded values and norms of the dominant communication technologies. The tactics that alternative communities use to make the Internet meet their local needs reveal the diverse possibilities for building and using technologies that offer crucial means of communication and community.

Appendix: Methodological Notes

Research for this book was conducted over many years and with a number of collaborators. I did not enter into these research projects with the intent of writing a book. Instead, while conducting research on Brooklyn's drag community, I began thinking about how I could build an analysis of countercultural communities and their relationships to digital technologies that could connect to my previous research. This appendix describes how I gathered data during a multiyear process of doing qualitative work with three separate countercultural communities. My interpretive framework grew out of sustained reengagement with my fieldwork, follow-up interviews, and data collection. In the following paragraphs, I describe the fieldwork that was undertaken for this book, followed by a brief discussion of coding.

BME

Chapter 3 discusses the online body modification community *Body Modification Ezine* (BME). My research on BME began as part of an internship with the Social Media Collective at Microsoft Research. In particular, I worked with danah boyd, a principal researcher there. I wanted to understand how people circulate information about radical or *extreme body modification* (EBM), which I defined as "body modification procedures that are unusual, permanent, and typically painful, including split tongues, ear pointing, silicone or magnetic implants, and the voluntary amputation of limbs and organs." Because these practices operate in a legal gray area, studying EBM can be as much of a project of social capital as a project of information.

Unlike the New Brunswick punk music community and the Brooklyn drag queen community, the body modification community is not tied to a specific geographic location, and I deliberately gathered as diverse a group as possible, eventually conducting interviews in several states in the United States and in Canada, New Zealand, and the United Kingdom. Interviews were originally conducted in 2011, primarily in person but occasionally by telephone or text-based chat (see table A.1). Because my definition of the field includes both online and offline contexts, participant observation for IAM included reading participants' modification-related blogs, hanging out at local piercing shops, and attending an annual campout for people in the modified community. These sites provided opportunities for informal interviews that provided additional context and perspectives.

Table A.1

Interviewees from BME

Participant	Age	Location	Format
Chris	32	Arizona	Phone
Cora	20	Pennsylvania	Face to face
Gabriel	23	Colorado	Skype
Gwen	21	New Zealand	Instant message
Harley	28	New York	Face to face
Lazarus	28	United Kingdom	Skype
Mark	30	Ontario, Canada	Skype
Memo	25	California	Face to face
Mike	41	Massachusetts	Face to face
Mr. Pink	28	Tennessee	Skype
Nick	28	Illinois	Skype
Oliver	25	Arizona	Phone
Paige	22	Quebec, Canada	Skype
Pixie	40	Oregon	Skype
Rachel	35	South Carolina	Phone
Randy	27	Michigan	Skype
Raskin	21	Ohio	Skype
Rhoda	25	New York	Face to face
Sean	37	Pennsylvania	Face to face
Tat	23	Missouri	Skype

Note: This table presents details about interviewees from the BME community. With the exception of Rachel Larratt, pseudonyms (chosen by participants) are used to provide confidentiality.

As I note in chapter 3, I have been a member of this online community for over a decade, after first encountering BME in high school while searching for information on piercings and scarification. Studying one's own community is always tricky, and involves striking a balance between reflexivity, objectivity, and longstanding familiarity with a community. In writing about BME for this book, I wanted to share a history of community that I both value and hold in suspicion, and I hope that both the values and criticisms of BME and IAM emerge with clarity in this analysis. I document some of the methodological issues in that project elsewhere (Lingel 2012).

Even while conducting interviews about extreme body modification and information poverty, I knew I wanted to offer a broader account of BME as a community. Compared to many of the currently dominant social media platforms, BME has a long online history, and I had seen it struggle to survive the emergence of mainstream sites. I returned to these interviews to develop an account of how BME developed as a community, particularly in terms of managing membership and maintaining a sense of alterity. I felt lucky to have conducted research on IAM in 2011, when the community was still fairly active, and follow-up interviews allowed me to understand how the 2011 redesign radically changed the appearance of IAM and became a kind of scapegoat for its decline. Learning about these struggles was productive for understanding community, but it also meant that IAM was something of a moving target in terms of recruiting or even developing a consistent interview protocol (see Pearce and Artemesia 2009 on the challenges of researching a community with an unstable platform). In 2014 and 2015, I conducted an additional set of interviews, with both former and new participants, including Rachel Larratt, the site's current owner. In keeping with longstanding conventions in social science research, Rachel is the only participant who (with her consent) was not assigned a pseudonym because it would be impossible to talk about the role that she played in the community without revealing her name.

Follow-up interviews allowed me to talk about the ways that IAM had changed since my first round of interviews in 2011 and also allowed me to solicit feedback as a form of member checks (Creswell and Clark 2007, 217). One thing that I wanted feedback on was whether to cite BME and IAM by name rather than pseudonym. My 2013 article with danah boyd gave the BME site a pseudonym, following standard conventions for occluding research sites. After the article was published, however, several participants and community members expressed disappointment with this decision. They felt that I had disrespected the community by changing the name, and in one case, a participant who was also a friend of nearly a decade explained (not unkindly) that he felt so strongly about identifying BME and IAM by name that he would both end our friendship and publicly condemn any future related research if I continued to use a pseudonym for the sites. This conversation was certainly a turning point in my thinking about how to handle naming and occlusion, but I could not let one person's beliefs dictate my decision, even if it was a longstanding friend in the community. I reached out to participants I had interviewed to poll their feelings on the issue, and without exception, they supported the decision to use BME's name, with the understanding that I would continue to use pseudonyms for participants themselves.

I turned to methods literature to think through this issue more thoroughly. Christina Dunbar-Hester's (2014) ethnographic work on radio activism provided a model, in that she also shifted from a pseudonym to the actual name of the organization she studied as she shifted from a journal article to a monograph. In addition, Annette N. Markham's work on the ethics of Internet research (Markham 2005; Markham, Buchanan, and AoIR Ethics Working Committee 2012) and Christine Hine's (2015) research on online ethnography were helpful in thinking through the ethics of this decision. There were other pragmatic factors to consider, too. After conference presentations of this research, people would occasionally ask me, typically with a knowing wink, if I was talking about BME and IAM. Given that BME has been the largest and most popular site for body modification on the Internet, I perhaps should not have been surprised that the site name pseudonym proved to be transparent to many readers. Either for techies who know a lot about online culture and a little bit about body modification or for body modification enthusiasts who know at least a little about the Internet, people who read my work simply assumed that I was talking about BME. Finally, when I interviewed the current site owner, Rachel Larratt, in fall 2015, she gave her approval to having the site called by its actual name in my research, so I felt that I had covered my bases in terms of participants, former site owners, and current site users, supported by literature in ethnography and ethics. With all of these factors in mind, I decided to list the site by name.

New Brunswick

Research on the New Brunswick, New Jersey, punk community began in fall 2009, shortly after I moved to New Jersey to start a PhD program at Rutgers University. Having loved punk and indie music since high school, I was surprised that a college town had very few local venues for live music. When I moved to nearby Highland Park, only one venue in New Brunswick offered shows to the under-twenty-one crowd, unlike other U.S. college towns like Madison, Lawrence, and Bloomington. My friend Aaron Trammel (a fellow grad student, a musician, and a longtime New Jersey resident) explained that New Brunswick music shows were tied to a network of houses that operated as DIY venues, and after much discussion, we realized that this was not just an entertainment problem; it was an information problem. We eventually teamed up with Nathan Graham, Joe Sanchez, and Mor Naaman to study the community as a sociotechnical phenomenon. More than the other two field studies included in this book, research on the New Brunswick punk community grew out of a deeply collaborative effort, and I am particularly grateful to Aaron Trammell for his advice and feedback throughout the first part of this project, which I would not have been able to develop further without his support and encouragement.

Researching the basement community had three basic parts—participant observation, a focus group, and individual interviews. Participant observations included going to shows and hanging out in bars, which we did collectively in 2009 and 2010 and I did on my own in 2014 and 2015. After we attended a show, went to an established alternate social hub (such as a bar), or casually bumped into a member of the scene, we took scratch notes that we later transcribed into more detailed field note accounts. As a team, we compiled field notes from dozens of hours of fieldwork in these various locations. Informal interviews were conducted during field observation, and these helped to shape guidelines for interview guides for both focus groups and individual interviews. To get a sense of the community's history and evolving practices, we used purposive sampling (Babbie 2010, 193) to conduct interviews with four individuals whose experiences with the community spanned four decades.

After many weeks of attending shows and conducting preliminary, semi-structured interviews with individual community members, we recruited participants for a focus group in fall 2009. The focus group was held for two hours with ten participants who had been active in the community for a number of years. Many had been involved with the scene since their teenage years. We saw the focus group as a way of delving into practices that we had observed in the community, such as locating venues by using code names and ask-a-punk. We asked about these practices as well as different communication platforms, including cell phone use, social media, zines, and message boards. The focus group gave us a rich understanding of the community and its relationships to secrecy and technology.

In fall 2010, Aaron Trammel and I conducted a second round of interviews, concentrating on how fans learned about upcoming shows rather than how show organizers sought to distribute information. Initially, we attempted to limit our interview pool solely to fans in the scene rather than band members or show promoters, who constituted focus group participants. Starting with contacts made through field observations, we used snowball sampling to extend our interview pool. As we conducted interviews, we found that limiting interviews solely to fans was challenging, not because it was difficult to locate fans in the scene but because roles of participation in the basement community are extremely fluid. The lines between living in a house where shows are conducted and promoting shows or between organizing events in the past and continuing to attend shows in the present turned out to be both fuzzy and malleable. Table A.2 provides details of our participants' demographic details and roles in the community.

Aaron, Joe, Mor, and I published a short paper in *CSCW 2012* about the use of social media and practices of secrecy (Lingel, Trammell, Sanchez, and Naaman 2012), but there was no way to work through the many sociotechnical tensions within the community in a four-page human-computer interaction paper. In returning to the interview data to write this book, I wanted to provide richer descriptions of the community and develop a more extensive analysis of secrecy, information practices, and sociotechnical tactics.

As was the case with BME, I struggled with whether to name the location of the basement community. In our *CSCW 2012* paper, our group listed the location because we agreed that New Brunswick's geography and its relationship to Rutgers was too essential to explaining the information practices to anonymize. The recent publication of a book about the basement

Table A.2
Interviewees from the New Brunswick, New Jersey, punk music community

Participant	Sex	Role	Age
Amanda	F	Fan	24
Lowell	M	Fan	23
Brady	M	Fan	26
Matt	M	Band	26
Tim	M	Promoter	24
Midori	F	Band	21
Mahdu	M	Band	28
Warren	M	House member	19
Lacey	F	Fan	19
Matilda	F	Fan	20

Note: This table presents details semistructured interviews that were conducted in fall 2010. The column titled "Role" shows the different modes of participating in the community—as band member, fan, member of a house where shows take place, and show promoter. In many cases, these roles overlap, in which case I use the term that dominated (but did not necessarily encompass) the interviewee's main mode of participating in the community.

community (*New Brunswick, New Jersey, Goodbye*) also served as a kind of precedent for our research.

Of the three field studies, the most time lapsed between New Brunswick fieldwork and publication. To some extent, it is impossible to have a comparative book of field studies that does not involve a time lag, in that the length of time required to conduct fieldwork, analyze data, write, and publish makes it inevitable that the analysis of (at least) one of the case studies will involve older data. I wanted members of the community to know that I was writing new analysis about New Brunswick punk, and the best way to circulate that information seemed to be via a zine. Zines have a long history in punk and DIY circles, and although I had not seen a significant number while conducting fieldwork, a zine seemed to be a way of communicating my respect for DIY values. My zine (called *Asking the Punks: A Basement Ethnography*) explained the research project and how it fit into the book. I listed my contact information in the zine and asked for feedback, questions, and concerns. In December 2014 and April 2015, I attended a number of basement shows in New Brunswick and distributed around a hundred copies of the zine. I was both relieved and disappointed that no one contacted me after seeing the zine. On the one hand, it meant that no one was so upset by my plans that I would have to reevaluate how or whether to include the field study in the book. On the other, it meant that I had not opened a new line of dialogue as far as member checks. Nevertheless, I feel it was a worthwhile approach in signaling to participants that I was still conducting work on their community.

Bushwick

My research into Brooklyn's drag community began through a collaboration with Adam Golub, who at the time had just earned a master of arts degree in journalism at Columbia University. After Adam completed a documentary film on the community in 2012 as part of his graduate work, he approached me about applying for a grant from the Brown Institute for Media Innovation, which supports research at the convergence of storytelling and technology. The grant allowed us to conduct focus groups with Brooklyn-based drag queens, focusing on the use of social media. Throughout our project, we had the support of administrators and other grantees at the Brown Institute, particularly Mark Hansen and Michael Krisch.

Because we were interested in the sociotechnical dimensions of drag, especially through social media, we felt that focus groups were a particularly useful methodological tool. Between September and December 2013, we conducted four focus groups with a total of fifteen participants. Groups ranged in size from two to five participants. Although the number of participants is small, our focus group populations represent a sizable percentage of Brooklyn's drag community, which included approximately a hundred active performers. We recruited participants through word-of-mouth and snowball sampling. Most participants knew each other, some intimately and others vaguely or by reputation. Participants had various levels of experience as performers: some were instrumental in creating Brooklyn's drag community, and others had begun performing only in the previous few months. All participants lived in Brooklyn, and they all were between twenty-four and thirty-five years old. To respect the fluidity of gender and sexuality prevalent in the drag community, we did not ask participants to list their sexuality, gender, or sex as part of our recruitment process. But during our conversations, several participants identified themselves as trans, which supports a narrative we encountered during fieldwork that Brooklyn's drag community sought to be inclusive and welcoming of trans performers. Focus group questions centered on the role that was played by social media for performers and as a tool of forming community. We also asked about the extent to which these practices had changed over time for performers who had participated in the scene for a number of years.

In addition to focus groups, we took advantage of a three-day salon called Drag Arts (held in Manhattan's Lower East Side in November 2013) to hold a workshop on the role that was played by social media in Brooklyn's drag community. The workshop drew approximately forty people, including drag performers (from Brooklyn and Manhattan) and nightlife goers. The workshop was structured as a moderated discussion of the themes that emerged from focus groups, including the role played by social media in promotion, documentation, and communication between performers and fans. We also addressed terminology as it relates to collective identity, working through collective understandings of terms like *community*, *subculture*, and *counterculture*. The workshop both supplemented our data and acted as a form of member checking (Creswell and Clark 2007, 217) because we were able to present some of the high-level themes from our interviews to a larger part of the community and solicit feedback.

Based on this research, Adam and I published an article in the *Journal of Computer Mediated Communication* (Lingel and Golub 2015) that concentrated on online identity work in the context of drag queens' everyday online lives. As was the case with the other two field studies in this book, many research avenues (particularly around issues of community) could not be pursued within the limits of the *JCMC* article. To explore how Brooklyn drag queens were making sense of Facebook's real-name/authentic-name policy, I conducted a small number of follow-up interviews and interviewed new participants whose accounts were frozen. I also incorporated textual analysis of Facebook activity as a source of data on the role played by social media in everyday life. I concentrated on a two-month period before and after the Bushwig 2015 festival, tracking social interactions and messages among queens I befriended during fieldwork.

An interesting dynamic unfolded in 2015 after I gave a talk presenting initial research from this fieldwork. An audience member introduced herself as a Facebook researcher and offered to be a point of contact for queens in my participant network who encountered problems with their accounts.

After I relayed this information to my participants, several of them later reached out to me with requests to help queens whose accounts had been frozen. After putting these performers in touch with my contact at Facebook, I asked if I could interview them about their relationship to Facebook and social media. For most of the queens I encountered this way, the most frustrating part of having their accounts frozen was feeling that they lacked recourse for addressing the alleged policy violation, making it particularly gratifying to provide a meaningful service within the community I had studied.

Data Analysis

In returning to this data with the intent of writing a book, my first step was to survey all the data that I had accumulated from prior fieldwork. I took notes on themes that emerged, concentrating on high-level issues that I knew I wanted to pursue in the book—alterity, community, and relationships to digital media. I then made a plan for additional data sources that would be required to engage these topics thoroughly, including follow-up interviews, textual analysis of social media content, and participant observation. After I conducted additional fieldwork, I recoded all transcripts and media. This meant setting aside the coding structures that I used in journal articles and reevaluating my sources in light of the new project. I used NVIVO software, drawing on an emic/etic approach (Miles, Huberman, and Saldana 2013). This approach to coding involves a simple, hierarchical structure of high-level themes identified by the researcher (etic), with codes nested below corresponding to how participants refer to these concepts (emic). For example, I was interested in the relationships between authenticity and alterity. Under the etic code authenticity, I eventually included subcodes like "sellout" and "scene points."

Emic/etic analysis provides a dialectical structure that puts concepts into conversation with (or perhaps more precisely, translated through) the terms and perspectives of participants. In addition, I used an open coding method (Corbin and Strauss 2015) to develop a set of codes that do not necessarily fall within the scope of etic themes but were interesting to me. In combination, the coding methods provide both structure and flexibility for developing observations and theoretical claims. After completing this new round of coding, I began developing the three-part framework that anchors the analytical component of my networked field studies method. Perhaps more than anything else, the coding process began to bind three distinct field sites into a cohesive conceptual project.

As a means of evaluating my analytical claims, I decided to conduct member checks, which involves soliciting feedback from participants on drafts or high-level themes. This was easiest for BME because I had the longest ties to this community. In fall 2014, I asked my interviewees and a few longtime IAM friends if they would read a draft of the chapter. I also asked a handful of participants from Brooklyn's drag community for feedback. Most responded positively, but few sent any substantive comments about my analysis. A better approach, I found, was to send an email or Facebook message to individuals or small groups of friends and include a short list of questions.

For example, in fall 2015, I sent a set of questions to a number of drag queen participants. Part of my interest in Brooklyn drag had to do with space, both in terms of safe spaces and New York City as a locus of queer culture. I had assumed that there would be at least some concerns about moving Bushwig from Brooklyn to Queens in 2015, given how many participants had clearly and forcefully claimed themselves as belonging not just to New York but to Brooklyn. But in asking for feedback on the arguments that I had made on the topic, participants indicated that I was making too much out of what they perceived to be a pragmatic decision to find a bigger, cheaper space that was slightly over the Brooklyn border. It was more difficult to conduct member checks in the New Brunswick punk music basement community, so I relied on feedback in casual conversations among people in my social network who were current or former members of the community.

As a whole, I found that thinking of member checks as a guided discussion about specific questions or doubts worked better than asking for wholesale feedback. The process was valuable for me in trying to ensure that participants had a mechanism for engaging with and critiquing my analysis of their communities.

Notes

Chapter 1: Introduction

1. Choosing a term to use for talking about groups of people is a problem that is familiar to many social theorists. For example, Ryan Moore (2005, 201) rejects the word *subculture* as being inadequate for describing the fluidity of the groups that he studied and uses the word *scene*, which he defines as "cultural, social, temporal and spatial zones in which diverse people interact and contest the meanings of their actions" (see also Pfadenhauer 2005). Similarly, Andy Bennett (1999) argues that the word *subculture* lacks flexibility and suggests thinking in terms of sociality and tribe relations. Lisa W. Loutzenheiser (2007, 121) argues that the lack of flexibility in the word *community* has to do primarily with the inability to reflect changing group ideology and instead suggests a cohesion that is in fact imaginary. See also Laura Portwood-Stacer (2013, 7) on the decision to shift between the words *subculture, movement, scene, milieu,* and *community* in her discussion of anarchist lifestyle politics.

2. I am essentially mapping these terms onto Raymond Williams's (1991) division of politics of difference.

3. For a helpful review of these debates in the 1990s, see Barry Wellman (1997). For other important critiques of community in anthropology and information science, see Vered Amit and Nigel Rapport (2002) and Tiffany C. Veinot and Kate Williams (2012), respectively.

4. I use the word *shape* here to point to social shaping theory of the relationships between technology and people. For a helpful review of social shaping theory (particularly in contrast to more determinist arguments), see Nancy Baym (2015).

5. There are real differences in people's relationships to outsider status. For some people, that status comes primarily from belonging to countercultural communities, and for other people (such as people of color, the very poor, and people who are differently abled), that status comes from participating in structural conditions of exclusion. Although the kinds of alterity that I study are often considered to be

choices, I am wary of assigning that label because many people in countercultural communities do not experience their participation as a choice. For example, consider the response of a drag performer to a question about when she first started doing drag: "I started doing drag in 1989 when I was born. … I *am* my drag persona, I guess." Similarly, many members of the body modification community see their physical alterations as part of a journey of self-expression that feels less like choice and more like a fulfillment of the person that they are meant to be, and they see their communities of alterity as vital resources for supporting that identity. Nevertheless, I recognize that a legitimate criticism of this book is the decision to use theories of alterity as applied to a narrow set of marginalized identities, leaving out structural and categorical experiences of marginalization.

6. I am grateful to Megan Finn for first pointing this out to me.

7. For a thorough treatment of what constitutes online ethnography, see Tom Boellstorff, Bonnie Nardi, Celia Pierce and T. L. Taylor (2012) and Christine Hine (2015).

8. These issues also emerge in the more extreme forms of body modification (Lingel and boyd, 2013) and are relevant to many other communities of alterity, such as sex workers (Grant 2014) and radical activists (Bratich 2011).

Chapter 2: Frameworks for Technology and Communities of Alterity

1. From this viewpoint, we might look at the punitive practice of doxing (from the abbreviation *docs* for *documents*), which is revealing identifying information about an anonymous or pseudonymous user as a form of forced authenticity or punishment.

2. For expanded reviews of these debates, see Baym 2015 and Hine 2015.

3. My favorite examples of technologies that were developed while people were seeking something else are tofu and gunpowder—both the result of the efforts of ancient Chinese alchemists who were seeking immortality (Jack 2015; Rupp 2014).

4. For useful edited collections on media activism, see Bart Cammaerts, Alice Mattoni, and Patrick McCurdy (2013) and Lina Dencik and Peter Wilkin (2015).

Chapter 3: The Death and Life of Great Online Subcultures

1. It is outside the scope of my analysis to compare the forms of body modification discussed in this chapter with cosmetic surgery like breast implants or liposuction. At first glance, the two sets of practices might seem opposite in terms of rejection of versus adherence to mainstream norms of beauty. Yet a reductive binary collapses with the increasing popularity of modifications like piercings and tattoos, and because extreme cases of cosmetic surgery can ultimately revolt rather than attract (Taussig 2012). As part of this investigation of alterity, I concentrate on body

modification as a set of practices that are associated with rejection of and by the mainstream. For further reading in this area, see Victoria Pitts-Taylor (2007) and Carl Elliott (2003).

2. For others, it is a religion. The Church of Body Modification is a nontheistic religion that claims to have 3,500 members in the United States. Its faith statement includes the following key tenets: "We will always respect our bodies. We believe it is our right to explore our world, both physical and supernatural, through spiritual body modification. We promise to always grow as individuals through body modification and what it can teach us about who we are and what we can do" (Church of Body Modification 2014). The church has been recognized as an official religion, both by the Internal Revenue Service in terms of tax status and in court cases where membership in the Church of Body Modification was used to protest discriminatory action by schools and employers (Netter 2010).

3. Several zines related to body modification included *Sacred Debris, I Am Not My Body,* and *Tatmag.* For an analysis of zines as forms of countercultural production, see Stephen Duncombe (1997) and Jenna Freedman (2006). Another connected form of media circulation can be found in pornography rings, where stigma becomes a driver in adopting secretive practices of circulating media (Wongsurawat 2005).

4. Title 18 of the United States Code is the country's criminal and penal code and includes laws on obscenity and photography. Paragraphs (b) and (c) of section 2252 govern digital images, domain names, and Internet content. Currently, twelve states (Alaska, California, Colorado, Georgia, Illinois, Iowa, Louisiana, Maine, Missouri, Oklahoma, South Carolina, and West Virginia) require film processors to be mandatory reporters. It is beyond the scope of this text to describe how these laws have changed over time (U.S. Department of Health and Human Services n.d.; U.S. Department of Justice n.d.). But it is useful to note that Sean references photo-processing laws that did not apply to his state of residence. Pointing to a legal threat that is tenuous to justify or explain an elaborate set of rules for communication also surfaces in the next chapter's discussion of New Brunswick punks and their relationships to the police.

5. For several years, rumors circulated that the Federal Bureau of Investigation was monitoring BME to document and track tattoos that were associated with gangs and domestic terrorists. After I submitted a Freedom of Information Act request form to the U.S. Department of Justice in 2014, asking for any materials related to Shannon Larratt or BMEzine.com LLC, I was informed that no such materials existed. Although the FBI surveillance rumors seem to have been unfounded, there are documented cases of police databases of modifications, such as Interpol's collaboration with the Centre for Anatomy and Human Identification to develop an image collection of piercings and tattoos (Lingel 2012).

6. There are essentially three ways that body modifications can run afoul of the law. First, health code violations are perhaps the most common concern. The Association

of Professional Piercers (APP) offers resources for dealing with state and, in some cases, city regulations for standards of business conduct for establishments offering body modification (Association of Professional Piercers 2012). Second, and far less common, are criminal assault charges or civil suits of misconduct, which have been virtually eliminated by the near-ubiquitous use (at least at reputable shops) of consent forms. Third, and pertaining to more extreme procedures, is the administration of subcutaneous anesthesia without a license. Although topical anesthesia may be administered without a license, injections may not. Practitioners who administer under-the-skin anesthesia thus run the risk of prosecution for practicing medical procedures without a license. For a journalistic account of some of these issues, see Jordan Ginsberg (2010).

7. Two URLs point to the same terms of service document: http://iam.bmezine.com\tos.html and http://iam.bmezine.com/viewdoc.exe?tos. The Wayback Machine captured 114 screenshots of the first URL between December, 5, 2001, and August 27, 2011, and thirty-seven screenshots of the second URL between October 20, 2002, and May 27, 2011.

8. http://wiki.bme.com/index.php?title=IAM_TOS.

9. A separate forum called "IAM: Deceased" exists for documenting users who have passed away. For these users, accounts are opened up to immediate family members, if requested.

10. There is a Facebook group for former IAM and BME members, where boundary politics persist in that moderators control group membership. In the second set of interviews that I conducted in 2014, I asked participants whether they had joined the Facebook group (most had) and what it meant to them. Paige's somewhat dismissive explanation was representative: "People just post their IAM membership name there. Then you can creep them on IAM *and* on Facebook."

Chapter 4: They Came from the Basement

1. Although I use the term *quasi-legal* to describe the activities of the basement community, I am ambivalent because I do not want to reinscribe the performances as illegal, thereby supporting the standpoint that shows should be shut down. My view is that basement shows do not endanger participants any more than the average college party and that attention to this community is driven by a view that punk aesthetics and politics are more threatening than, say, those of college fraternities, despite the many instances of danger and violence that occur at college fraternities and sororities (see Flanagan 2014). In interviews, participants discussed this comparison and the stakes that both university and city authorities had in shutting down the shows. I use the term *quasi-legal* when describing the basement community because these activities operate in a legal gray area and because legal

tenuousness is essential to how the community perceives itself, which has important consequences for my interests in practices of technology and information.

2. I am grateful to Joe Sanchez for pointing me to these discussion threads.

3. These message boards are not named here to protect the confidentiality of participants.

4. New Brunswick is not alone in dealing with police infiltration of an underground music scene. See Luke O'Neil (2013) for an account of how police used social media to locate house parties and shows in Boston. Philadelphia city council members took a different approach in 2016 when they proposed local legislation that would require musicians to register their personal information before booking a show (Slaughter 2016).

5. Although I attended many shows while conducting fieldwork, I never attended a show that was shut down by police. At the 2010 focus group, my collaborators and I asked the ten participants to talk about any occasions in which police had shut down shows, and they told us about only two instances. Moreover, participants admitted that these encounters were both positive. In one case, a police officer even jokingly requested that the band cover a favorite heavy metal song. Although in-person encounters were described positively, anxiety about the police persisted and was supported by widely circulated documentations of police attempts at social media subterfuge.

6. Light's (2014) arguments echo human-computer interaction research on use and users as a guiding paradigm in computer science, to the exclusion of other ways of relating to technology (see Satchell and Dourish 2009 and Baumer et al. 2015).

7. After fieldwork concluded, I heard of another instance of someone collecting show information and posting it online, this time on Twitter. I was unable to set up an interview with the account owner. Other members of the basement community have indicated that the account owner is a longtime community member, supporting my arguments that Tom's site failed partly because he lacked street credentials. In addition, the continued declining popularity of Myspace, which once was an important node of communication about local music, has encouraged experimentation with other platforms. At the time of writing, the Twitter account had under twenty followers.

8. I am grateful to David Grazian for making this point to me.

Chapter 5: Fight for Your Platform to Party

1. These transformations are not without consequences or local tensions. In the six weeks following the 2014 Bushwig festival, four seemingly unrelated hate crimes took place, all targeting trans or queer people (Miles 2014; Redmond 2014; Yaniv

and Paranscandola 2014). Although New York is celebrated as a home for queer culture, it is certainly not free from violence or discrimination against queer folk.

2. I originally assumed that performers would be interested in secrecy, at least in terms of keeping their drag activities or their queerness hidden from parts of their online networks. In interviews, this turned out not to be the case. Although many participants maintained multiple Facebook accounts, this tactic emerged out of a desire to keep their drag lives separate rather than secret. Many participants maintained what they called "boy pages" and "queen pages" because being a drag queen online (like being a drag queen offline) often involved a lot of work and they sometimes wanted to use Facebook simply to check on their friends and family without the flirting, teasing, and cajoling that they associated with maintaining queen pages.

3. In this chapter, I follow drag queens' tendency to refer to each other using feminine pronouns, irrespective of what their gender identity was or whether they were currently in drag. Because this chapter relies predominantly on focus groups rather than individual interviews, I do not use pseudonyms to refer to interviewees and instead describe them as Participant 1, 2, and so on.

4. This language of having a journey or narrative arc maps closely onto the discursive tendency in the body modification community to see modifications as part of an evolving journey (DeMello 2000).

5. I use the word *hospitality* in the sense that Roger Silverstone (2006) outlines in his arguments that hospitality is a condition of media that seeks to support a democratic and participatory dialogue.

References

Ahmed, S. 2000. *Strange Encounters: Embodied Others in Post-coloniality*. London: Routledge.

Ananny, M. 2011. "The Curious Connection between Apps for Gay Men and Sex Offenders." *The Atlantic*, April, http://www.theatlantic.com/technology/archive/2011/04/the-curious-connection-between-apps-for-gay-men-and-sex-offenders/237340.

Amit, V., and N. Rapport. 2002. *The Trouble with Community: Anthropological Reflections on Movement, Identity and Collectivity*. London: Pluto.

Association of Professional Piercers. 2012. "Legislation." http://www.safepiercing.org/legislation/legislation-links-by-state.

Babbie, E. R. 2010. *The Practice of Social Research*. Belmont, CA: Wadsworth.

Bailey, M. M. 2011. "Gender/Racial Realness: Theorizing the Gender System in Ballroom Culture." *Feminist Studies* 37 (2): 365–386.

Banet-Weiser, S. 2012. *Authentic TM: Politics and Ambivalence in a Brand Culture*. New York: NYU Press.

Barassi, V. 2015. *Activism on the Web: Everyday Struggles against Digital Capitalism*. New York: Routledge.

Baumer, E. P., P. Adams, V. D. Khovanskaya, T. C. Liao, M. E. Smith, V. Schwanda Sosik, and K. Williams. 2013. "Limiting, Leaving, and (Re)lapsing: An Exploration of Facebook Non-use Practices and Experiences." In *CHI '13: Proceedings of the SIGCHI Conference on Human Factors in Computing Systems*, 3257–3266. New York: ACM.

Baumer, E. P., J. Burrell, M. G. Ames, J. R. Brubaker, and P. Dourish. 2015. "On the Importance and Implications of Studying Technology Non-use." *Interactions* 22 (2): 52–56.

Baym, N. K. 2015. *Personal Connections in the Digital Age*. New York: Wiley.

Bell, M., and E. Flock. 2011. "'A Gay Girl in Damascus' Comes Clean." *Washington Post*, June 12, http://www.washingtonpost.com/lifestyle/style/a-gay-girl-in-damascus-comes-clean/2011/06/12/AGkyH0RH_story.html.

Benjamin, W. 2008. *The Work of Art in the Age of Mechanical Reproduction*. New York: Penguin Press. Originally published in 1935.

Bennett, A. 1999. "Subcultures or Neo-tribes? Rethinking the Relationship between Youth, Style and Musical Taste." *Sociology* 33 (3): 599–617.

Blanton, D. 2014. "Fox News Poll: Tattoos Aren't Just for Rebels Anymore." Fox News, March 14, http://www.foxnews.com/us/2014/03/14/fox-news-poll-tattoos-arent-just-for-rebels-anymore.

Boellstorff, T., B. Nardi, C. Pierce, and T. L. Taylor. 2012. *Ethnography and Virtual Worlds: A Handbook of Method*. Princeton, NJ: Princeton University Press.

Bossewitch, J., and A. Sinnreich. 2012. "The End of Forgetting: Strategic Agency beyond the Panopticon." *New Media and Society* 15 (2): 224–242.

Bourdieu, P. 2011. "The Forms of Capital." In *Cultural Theory: An Anthology*, ed. Imre Szeman and Timothy Kaposy, 81–93. Chichester, UK: Wiley-Blackwell.

Bowker, G., and S. Star. 1999. *Sorting Things Out: Classification and Its Consequences*. Cambridge, MA: MIT Press.

boyd, d. 2001. "Sexing the Internet: Reflections on the Role of Identification in Online Communities." CiteSeer, http://citeseerx.ist.psu.edu/viewdoc/summary?doi=10.1.1.58.4412.

boyd, d. 2006. "Friends, Friendsters, and Myspace Top 8: Writing Community into Being on Social Network Sites." *First Monday*, http://firstmonday.org/article/view/1418/1336.

boyd, d. 2012. "The Politics of Real Names." *Communications of the ACM* 55 (8): 29–31.

boyd, d. 2014. *It's Complicated: The Social Lives of Networked Teens*. New Haven, CT: Yale University Press.

boyd, d., and N. Ellison. 2013. "Sociality through Social Network Sites." In *The Oxford Handbook of Internet Studies*, ed. W. H. Dutton, 151–172. Oxford: Oxford University Press.

boyd, d., and A. Marwick. 2011. "Why Cyberbullying Rhetoric Misses the Mark." *New York Times*, September 22, http://www.nytimes.com/2011/09/23/opinion/why-cyberbullying-rhetoric-misses-the-mark.html.

Bratich, J. 2011. "User-Generated Discontent: Convergence, Polemology and Dissent." *Cultural Studies* 25 (4–5): 621–640.

Brunton, F. 2013. *Spam: A Shadow History of the Internet*. Cambridge, MA: MIT Press.

Brunton, F., and H. Nissenbaum. 2015. *Obfuscation: A User's Guide for Privacy and Protest*. Cambridge, MA: MIT Press.

Burrell, J. 2012. *Invisible Users: Youth in the Internet Cafés of Urban Ghana*. Cambridge, MA: MIT Press.

Bushwig. 2014. "About." Bushwig.com, http://www.bushwig.com/2013-2.

Cammaerts, B., A. Mattoni, and P. McCurdy. 2013. *Mediation and Protest Movements*. Bristol, UK: Intellect Books.

Change.org. 2014. "Allow Performers to Use Their Stage Names on Their Facebook Accounts!" Change.org, https://www.change.org/p/facebook-allow-performers-to-use-their-stage-names-on-their-facebook-accounts.

Chatman, E. A. 1991. "Life in a Small World: Applicability of Gratification Theory to Information-Seeking Behavior." *Journal of the American Society for Information Science* 42 (6): 438–449.

Chatman, E. A. 1999. "A Theory of Life in the Round." *Journal of the American Society for Information Science* 50 (3): 207–217.

Chun, W.H.K. 2006. *Control and Freedom: Power and Paranoia in the Age of Fiber Optics*. Cambridge, MA: MIT Press.

Church of Body Modification. 2014. "Statement of Faith." Church of Body Modification, http://uscobm.com/statement-of-faith.

Clark, R. Forthcoming. "Building a Digital Girl Army: Cultivating Feminist Safe Spaces Online."

Cohen, J. E. 2012. *Configuring the Networked Self: Law, Code, and the Play of Everyday Practice*. New Haven, CT: Yale University Press.

Coleman, B. 2011. *Hello Avatar: Rise of the Networked Generation*. Cambridge, MA: MIT Press.

Collins, M. 2013. "Smartphone Use While Walking Is Painfully Dumb." *Scientific American*, November 19, http://www.scientificamerican.com/article/smartphone-use-while-walking-is-painfully-dumb.

Corbin, J., and A. Strauss. 2015. *Basics of Qualitative Analysis: Techniques and Procedures for Developing Grounded Theory*. Los Angeles: Sage.

Costanza-Chock, S. 2014. *Out of the Shadows, into the Streets! Transmedia Organizing and the Immigrant Rights Movement*. Cambridge, MA: MIT Press.

Couldry, N. 2004. "Theorising Media as Practice." *Social Semiotics* 14 (2): 115–132.

Couldry, N., and J. Turow. 2014. "Advertising, Big Data and the Clearance of the Public Realm: Marketers' New Approaches to the Content Subsidy." *International Journal of Communication* 8: 1710–1726.

Crawford, K. 2013. "The Hidden Biases in Big Data." *Harvard Business Review*, https://hbr.org/2013/04/the-hidden-biases-in-big-data.

Crawford, K., and T. Gillespie. 2014. "What Is a Flag For? Social Media Reporting Tools and the Vocabulary of Complaint." *New Media and Society* 18 (3): 410–428.

Crawford, M. B. 2009. *The Case for Working with Your Hands, or, Why Office Work Is Bad for Us and Fixing Things Feels Good*. London: Viking.

Creswell, J. W., and V. L. Plano Clark. 2007. *Designing and Conducting Mixed Methods Research*. Thousand Oaks, CA: Sage.

Dalbello, M. 2004. "Institutional Shaping of Cultural Memory: Digital Library as Environment for Textual Transmission1." *Library* 74 (3): 265–298.

De Certeau, M. 1984. *The Practice of Everyday Life*. Berkeley: University of California Press.

DeMello, M. 2000. *Bodies of Inscription: A Cultural History of the Modern Tattoo Community*. Durham, NC: Duke University Press.

Dencik, L., and P. Wilkin. 2015. *Worker Resistance and Media*. New York: Lang.

Denzin, N. K., and Y. S. Lincoln. 2000. *Handbook of Qualitative Research*. Thousand Oaks, CA: Sage.

Dibbell, J. 1998. *My Tiny Life: Crime and Passion in a Virtual World*. New York: Holt.

Douglas, M. 1991. *Purity and Danger: An Analysis of the Concepts of Pollution and Taboo*. London: Routledge.

Dourish, P., R. E. Grinter, J. Delgado de la Flor, and M. Joseph. 2004. "Security in the Wild: User Strategies for Managing Security as an Everyday, Practical Problem." *Personal and Ubiquitous Computing* 8: 391–401.

Drabinski, E. 2013. "Queering the Catalog: Queer Theory and the Politics of Correction." *The Library Quarterly: Information, Community, Policy* 83 (2): 94–111.

Driscoll, K. 2014. "Hobbyist Inter-Networking and the Popular Internet Imaginary: Forgotten Histories of Networked Personal Computing, 1978–1998." PhD diss., University of Southern California.

Druick, Z. 1995. "The Information Superhighway, or the Politics of a Metaphor." *Bad Subjects* 18.

Dunbar-Hester, C. 2010. "Beyond 'Dudecore'? Challenging Gendered and 'Raced' Technologies through Media Activism." *Journal of Broadcasting and Electronic Media* 54 (1): 121–135.

Dunbar-Hester, C. 2014. *Low Power to the People: Pirates, Politics and Protest in Radio Activism*. Cambridge, MA: MIT Press.

Duncombe, S. 1997. *Notes from Underground: Zines and the Politics of Alternative Culture*. New York: Verso.

Eglash, R., J. Croissant, G. Di Chiro, and R. Fouché, eds. 2004. *Appropriating Technology: Vernacular Science and Social Power*. Minneapolis: University of Minnesota Press.

Elliott, C. 2003. *Better Than Well: American Medicine Meets the American Dream*. New York: Norton.

Eslami, M., A. Rickman, K. Vaccaro, A. Aleyasen, A. Vuong, K. Karahalios, K. Hamilton, and C. Sandvig. 2015. "I Always Assumed That I Wasn't Really That Close to [Her]: Reasoning about Invisible Algorithms in News Feeds." In *Proceedings of the 33rd Annual ACM Conference on Human Factors in Computing Systems*, 153–162. New York: ACM.

Eubanks, V. 2011. *Digital Dead End: Fighting for Social Justice in the Information Age*. Cambridge, MA: MIT Press.

Facebook. 2015. "What Types of ID Does Facebook Accept?" Facebook.com, https://www.facebook.com/help/159096464162185.

Facebook. 2016. "Community Standards." Facebook.com, https://www.facebook.com/communitystandards.

Fine, G. A., and L. Holyfield. 1996. "Secrecy, Trust, and Dangerous Leisure: Generating Group Cohesion in Voluntary Organizations." *Social Psychology Quarterly* 59 (1): 22–38.

Fiske, J. 1995. "Popular Culture." In *Critical Terms for Literary Study*, 2nd ed., ed. Frank Lentricchia and Thomas McLaughlin, 2, 321–335. Chicago: University of Chicago Press.

Flanagan, C. 2014. "The Dark Power of Fraternities." *The Atlantic*, http://www.theatlantic.com/features/archive/2014/02/the-dark-power-of-fraternities/357580.

Flichy, P. 2007. *The Internet Imaginaire*. Cambridge, MA: MIT Press.

Fox, S., R. R. Ulgado, and D. Rosner. 2015. "Hacking Culture, Not Devices: Access and Recognition in Feminist Hackerspaces." In *CSCW '15: Proceedings of the Eighteenth ACM Conference on Computer Supported Cooperative Work and Social Computing*, ed. Dan Cosley and Andrea Forte, 56–68. New York: ACM Press.

Freedman, J. 2006. "A DIY Collection." *Library Journal* 131 (11): 36–38.

Garland-Thomson, R. 2011. "Misfits: A Feminist Materialist Disability Concept." *Hypatia* 26 (3): 591–609.

Gehl, R. W. 2014. *Reverse Engineering Social Media: Software, Culture, and Political Economy in New Media Capitalism*. Philadelphia, PA: Temple University Press.

Gelber, S. 1997. "Do-It-Yourself: Constructing, Repairing, and Maintaining Domestic Masculinity." *American Quarterly* 49 (1): 66–112.

Gillespie, T. 2010. "The Politics of Platforms." *New Media and Society* 12 (3): 347–364.

Ginsberg, J. 2010. "Inside the Bloody World of Illegal Plastic Surgery." *This*, http://this.org/magazine/2010/11/25/the-cutter.

Goodman, E., and J. Vertesi. 2012. "Design for x? Distribution Choices and Ethical Design." *CHI'12: Extended Abstracts on Human Factors in Computing Systems*, 81–90. New York: ACM.

Graham, M. 2013. "Geography/Internet: Ethereal Alternate Dimensions of Cyberspace or Grounded Augmented Realities." *The Geographical Journal*, http://papers.ssrn.com/sol3/papers.cfm?abstract_id=2166874.

Grant, M. G. 2014. *Playing the Whore: The Work of Sex Work*. New York: Verso.

Grasmuck, S., J. Martin, and S. Zhao. 2009. "Ethno-Racial Identity Displays on Facebook." *Journal of Computer-Mediated Communication* 15 (1): 158–188.

Gregg, M. 2011. *Work's Intimacy*. Cambridge, UK: Polity.

Gutman, M., and J. Haskell. 2013. "Rebecca Sedwick Suicide: Parents of Alleged Cyberbully Blame Facebook Hack." *ABC News*, October 16, http://abcnews.go.com/US/parents-alleged-rebecca-sedwick-cyberbully-blame-facebook-hack/story?id=20583537.

Haimson, O. L., J. R. Brubaker, L. Dombrowski, and G. R. Hayes. 2016. "Digital Footprints and Changing Networks during Online Identity Transitions." In *CHI '16: Proceedings of the 2016 CHI Conference on Human Factors in Computing Systems*, ed. Jofish Kaye and Allison Druin,1176–1190. New York: ACM.

Haimson, O. L., and L. Hoffmann. 2016. "Constructing and Enforcing 'Authentic' Identity Online: Facebook, Real Names, and Non-normative Identities." *First Monday* 21 (6), http://firstmonday.org/ojs/index.php/fm/article/view/6791/5521.

Halperin, D. M. 1997. *Saint Foucault: Towards a Gay Hagiography*. New York: Oxford University Press.

Hamer, J. S. 2003. "Coming-Out: Gay Males' Information Seeking." *School Libraries Worldwide* 9 (2): 73–89.

Harding, A. 2010. "Is Your Desk Job Bad for Your Health?" *CNN*, June 22, http://www.cnn.com/2010/HEALTH/06/22/desk.job.bad.health/index.html.

Harrison, S., and P. Dourish. 1996. "Re-place-ing Space: The Roles of Place and Space in Collaborative Systems." In *Proceedings of the 1996 ACM Conference on Computer*

Supported Cooperative Work (CSCW '96), ed. Gary Olson and Judy Olson, 67–76. New York: ACM. http://www.dourish.com/publications/1996/cscw96-place.pdf.

Hassan, R. 2007. "Network Time." In *24/7: Time and Temporality in Network Society*, ed. R. Hassan and R. Purser, 37–61. Stanford, CA: Stanford University Press.

Hebdige, D. 1995. "Subculture: The Meaning of Style." *Critical Quarterly* 37 (2): 120–124.

Hine, C. 2015. *Ethnography for the Internet: Embedded, Embodied, and Everyday*. London: Bloomsbury Press.

Hodkinson, P. 2002. *Goth: Identity, Style, and Subculture*. Oxford: Berg.

Hogan, B. 2010. "The Presentation of Self in the Age of Social Media: Distinguishing Performances and Exhibitions Online." *Bulletin of Science, Technology & Society* 30 (6): 377–386.

Holpuch, A. 2015. "Facebook Adjusts Controversial 'Real Name' Policy in Wake of Criticism." *The Guardian*, December 15, http://www.theguardian.com/us-news/2015/dec/15/facebook-change-controversial-real-name-policy.

Jack, S. 2015. "Soy Story." *Eating China*, http://www.eatingchina.com/articles/soystory.htm.

Jaeger, P. T., and G. Burnett. 2010. *Information Worlds: Social Context, Technology, and Information Behavior in the Age of the Internet*. New York: Routledge.

Jenkins, H. 2006. *Convergence Culture: Where Old and New Media Collide*. New York: NYU Press.

Jenkins, H. 2013. *Textual Poachers: Television Fans and Participatory Culture*. New York: Routledge.

Jenkins, H., S. Ford, and J. Green. 2013. *Spreadable Media: Creating Value and Meaning in a Networked Culture*. New York: NYU Press.

Jones, G. M. 2014. "Secrecy." *Annual Review of Anthropology* 43 (1): 53–69.

Joseph, M. 2002. *Against the Romance of Community*. Minneapolis: University of Minnesota Press.

Kitchin, R., and M. Dodge. 2011. *Code/space: Software and Everyday Life*. Cambridge, MA: MIT Press.

Kranzberg, M. 1986. "Technology and History: Kranzberg's Laws." *Technology and Culture* 27 (3): 544–560.

Landemore, H. 2014. "We, All of the People." *Slate*, http://www.slate.com/articles/technology/future_tense/2014/07/five_lessons_from_iceland_s_failed_crowdsourced_constitution_experiment.html.

Larratt, S. 2012. "Facebook Is Not Your Friend." *ModBlog*, August 4, http://news.bme.com/2012/08/04/facebook-is-not-your-friend.

Light, B. 2014. *Disconnecting with Social Networking Sites*. New York: Springer.

Lingel, J. 2012. "The Life and Death of Our Research Data." *Social Media Collective*, February 9, http://socialmediacollective.org/2012/02/09/the-life-and-death-of-our-research-data.

Lingel, J., and d. boyd. 2013. "'Keep It Secret, Keep It Safe': Information Poverty, Information Norms, and Stigma." *Journal of the American Society for Information Science and Technology* 64 (5): 981–991.

Lingel, J., and A. Golub. 2015. "In Face on Facebook: Brooklyn's Drag Community and Sociotechnical Practices of Online Communication." *Journal of Computer-Mediated Communication* 20 (5): 536–553.

Lingel, J., A. Trammell, J. Sanchez, and M. Naaman. 2012. "Practices of Information and Secrecy in a Punk Rock Subculture." In Steven Poltrock and Carla Simone, eds., *CSCW '12: The 2012 ACM Conference on Computer Supported Cooperative Work*, 157–166. New York: ACM.

Litt, E. 2012. "Knock, Knock. Who's There? The Imagined Audience." *Journal of Broadcasting & Electronic Media* 56 (3): 330–345.

Liu, H. 2007. "Social Network Profiles as Taste Performances." *Journal of Computer Mediated Communication* 13 (1): 252–275.

Livingston, J., director. P. Gibson, cinematographer, and J. Oppenheim, editor. 2005. *Paris Is Burning*. 1990. Burbank, CA: Miramax Home Entertainment.

Livingstone, S. 2008. "Taking Risky Opportunities in Youthful Content Creation: Teenagers' Use of Social Networking Sites for Intimacy, Privacy and Self-Expression." *New Media and Society* 10 (3): 393–411.

Loutzenheiser, L. W. 2007. "Working Alterity: The Impossibility of Ethical Research with Youth." *Educational Studies* 41 (2): 109–127.

Lykke, N. 2010. *Feminist Studies: A Guide to Intersectional Theory, Methodology and Writing*. New York: Routledge.

Lyman, P. 1998. "The Poetics of the Future: Information Highways, Virtual Communities and Digital Libraries." Paper presented at the Lazerow Lecture Series, School of Library and Information Sciences, University of California, Los Angeles, http://www.freeebay.net/site/index2.php?option=com_content&do_pdf=1&id=369.

Ma, X., J. Hancock, and M. Naaman. 2016. "Anonymity, Intimacy and Self-Disclosure in Social Media." In *Proceedings of the 2016 CHI Conference on Human Factors in Computing Systems*, 3857–3869. New York: ACM.

Malin, B. J. 2014. *Feeling Mediated: A History of Media Technology and Emotion in America*. New York: New York University Press.

Manovich, L. 2009. "The Practice of Everyday (Media) Life: From Mass Consumption to Mass Cultural Production?" *Critical Inquiry* 35 (2): 319–331.

Marcus, G. E. 1995. "Ethnography in/of the World System: The Emergence of Multi-sited Ethnography." *Annual Review of Anthropology* 24: 95–117.

Markham, A. N. 2005. "The Methods, Politics, and Ethics of Representation in Online Ethnography." In *The Sage Handbook of Qualitative Research*, ed. N. Denzin and Y. Lincoln, 793–820. Thousand Oaks, CA: Sage.

Markham, A., E. Buchanan, and AoIR Ethics Working Committee. 2012. "Ethical Decision-making and Internet Research: Version 2.0." Association of Internet Researchers, http://www.uwstout.edu/ethicscenter/upload/aoirethicsprintablecopy.pdf.

Marvin, C. 1988. *When Old Technologies Were New*. Oxford, UK: Oxford University Press.

Marwick, A. E. 2008. "To Catch a Predator? The MySpace Moral Panic." *First Monday* 13 (6), http://firstmonday.org/ojs/index.php/fm/article/viewArticle/2152/1966.

Marwick, A. E. 2013. *Status Update: Celebrity, Publicity and Branding in the Social Media Age*. New Haven, CT: Yale University Press.

Marwick, A. E. 2014. "Networked Privacy: How Teenagers Negotiate Context on Social Media." *New Media and Society* 16 (7): 1051–1067.

Marwick, A., and d. boyd. 2011. "I Tweet Honestly, I Tweet Passionately: Twitter Users, Context Collapse, and the Imagined Audience." *New Media and Society* 13 (1): 114–133.

Marwick, A., and d. boyd. 2014. "'It's Just Drama': Teen Perspectives on Conflict and Aggression in a Networked Era." *Journal of Youth Studies* 17 (9): 1187–1204.

Masnick, M. 2012. "To Read All of the Privacy Policies You Encounter, You'd Need to Take a Month off from Work Each Year." *Tech Dirt*, https://www.techdirt.com/articles/20120420/10560418585/to-read-all-privacy-policies-you-encounter-youd-need-to-take-month-off-work-each-year.shtml.

Mazmanian, M. 2015. "'iCrazy': Positioning Self in Relationship to Time." Paper presented at the Annual Conference of the Society for the Social Studies of Science, November 11–15, Denver, CO, USA.

McGlotten, S. 2013. *Virtual Intimacies: Media, Affect, and Queer Sociality*. Albany: SUNY Press.

McMillan Cottom, T. 2014. "Democratizing Ideologies and Inequality Regimes in Digital Domains." Paper presented at the Berkman Center for Internet and Society Lecture Series, https://cyber.law.harvard.edu/events/luncheon/2014/07/cottom.

Merriam-Webster. 2014. "Stigma." Merriam-Webster.com, http://www.merriam-webster.com/dictionary/stigma.

Merrin, W. 2007. "Myspace and Legendary Psychasthenia." *Media Studies 2.0*, September 14, http://mediastudies2point0.blogspot.com/2007/09/myspace-and-legendary-psychasthenia.html.

Merten, D. E. 1999. "Enculturation into Secrecy among Junior High School Girls." *Journal of Contemporary Ethnography* 28 (2): 107–137.

Miaskiewicz, T., and K. A. Kozar. 2011. "Personas and User-Centered Design: How Can Personas Benefit Product Design Processes?" *Design Studies* 32 (5): 417–430.

Miles, D. 2014. "Suspect Indicted in Bushwick Transgender Shooting." WABC-TV New York, November 7, http://7online.com/news/suspect-indicted-in-bushwick-transgender-shooting/369731.

Miles, M. B., A. M. Huberman, and J. Saldana. 2013. *Qualitative Data Analysis: A Methods Sourcebook*. Thousand Oaks, CA: Sage.

Moore, R. 2005. "Alternative to What? Subcultural Capital and the Commercialization of a Music Scene." *Deviant Behavior* 26 (3): 229–252.

Muggleton, D. 2000. *Inside Subculture: The Postmodern Meaning of Style*. Oxford, UK: Berg.

Nakamura, L. 1995. "Race in/for Cyberspace: Identity Tourism and Racial Passing on the Internet." *Works and Days* 25 (26), http://mysite.du.edu/~lavita/edpx_3770_13s/_docs/nakamura_race_in_cyberspace.pdf.

Nakamura, L. 2013. *Cybertypes: Race, Ethnicity, and Identity on the Internet*. New York: Routledge.

Nardi, B. A. 2010. *My Life as a Night Elf Priest: An Anthropological Account of World of Warcraft*. Ann Arbor: University of Michigan Press.

Netter, S. 2010. "Student's Body Modification Religion Questioned after Nose Piercing Controversy." *ABC News*, September 16, http://abcnews.go.com/US/students-body-modification-religion-questioned-nose-piercing-controversy/story?id=11645847.

Newitz, A. 2005. "Dangerous Terms: A User's Guide to EULAs." Electronic Frontier Foundation, https://www.eff.org/wp/dangerous-terms-users-guide-eulas.

Newton, P. 2013. "Canadian Teen Commits Suicide after Alleged Rape, Bully." *CNN*, April 10, http://www.cnn.com/2013/04/10/justice/canada-teen-suicide/index.html.

Nissenbaum, H. 2010. *Privacy in Context: Technology, Policy and the Integrity of Social Life*. Stanford, CA: Stanford Law Books.

Occupy Wall Street. 2013. "On Consensus." OccupyWallStreet.org, http://occupywallst.org/article/on-consensus.

O'Neil, L. 2013. "Boston Punk Zombies Are Watching You." *Slate*, March 29, http://www.slate.com/articles/news_and_politics/crime/2013/03/boston_police_catfishing_indie_rockers_cops_pose_as_punks_on_the_internet.html.

Oudshoorn, N., and T. Pinch. 2005. *How Users Matter: The Co-construction of Users and Technologies*. Cambridge, MA: MIT Press.

Papacharissi, Z. 2011. *A Networked Self: Identity, Community, and Culture on Social Network Sites*. New York: Routledge.

Pariser, E. 2011. *The Filter Bubble: What the Internet Is Hiding from You*. New York: Penguin.

Pasquale, F. 2015. *The Black Box Society: The Secret Algorithms That Control Money and Information*. Cambridge, MA: Harvard University Press.

Pearce, C., and Artemesia. 2009. *Communities of Play: Emergent Cultures in Multiplayer Games and Virtual Worlds*. Cambridge, MA: MIT Press.

Perrin, A. 2015. "Social Media Usage: 2005–2015." Pew Research Center, http://www.pewinternet.org/2015/10/08/social-networking-usage-2005-2015.

Petrilli, M. J. 2012. "The Fifty Zip Codes with the Largest Growth in White Population Share, 2000–2010." *Flypaper*, http://foodandspice.blogspot.com/2014/08/green-pea-falafel.html.

Pfadenhauer, M. 2005. "Ethnography of Scenes: Towards a Sociological Life-World Analysis of (Post-traditional) Community-Building. *Forum: Qualitative Social Research / Sozialforschung* 6 (3): 1–15.

Philipson, A. 2014. "Email Is Dead for Today's Students Who Prefer Twitter, Universities Say." *The Telegraph*, May 30, http://www.telegraph.co.uk/technology/social-media/10864320/Email-is-dead-for-todays-students-who-prefer-Twitter-universities-say.html.

Phillip, A. 2015. "Online 'Authenticity' and How Facebook's 'Real Name' Policy Hurts Native Americans." *Washington Post*, February 10, https://www.washingtonpost.com/news/morning-mix/wp/2015/02/10/online-authenticity-and-how-facebooks-real-name-policy-hurts-native-americans.

Pickard, V. W. 2006. "United Yet Autonomous: Indymedia and the Struggle to Sustain a Radical Democratic Network." *Media Culture and Society* 28 (3): 315–336.

Pink, S. 2014. "Digital-Visual-Sensory Design Anthropology: Ethnography, Imagination and Intervention." *Arts and Humanities in Higher Education* 13 (4): 412–427.

Pitts-Taylor, V. 2007. *Surgery Junkies: Wellness and Pathology in Cosmetic Culture*. New Brunswick, NJ: Rutgers University Press.

Popkin, H. S. 2011. "Privacy Is Dead on Facebook, Get over It." NBC News, http://www.nbcnews.com/id/34825225/ns/technology_and_science-tech_and_gadgets/t/privacy-dead-facebook-get-over-it.

Portwood-Stacer, L. 2013. *Lifestyle Politics and Radical Activism*. New York: Bloomsbury Press.

Prost, A., and G. Vincent, eds. 1991. *A History of Private Life: Riddles of Identity in Modern Times*, vol. 5. Cambridge, MA: Belknap Press of Harvard University Press.

Pursell, C. 1993. "The Rise and Fall of the Appropriate Technology Movement in the United States, 1965–1985." *Technology and Culture* 34 (3): 629–637.

Ratto, M., and M. Boler, eds. 2014. *DIY Citizenship: Critical Making and Social Media*. Cambridge, MA: MIT Press.

Redmond, J. 2014. "Three Arrested in Connection with Anti-gay Attack, Shooting in Brooklyn." *Towleroad*, September 29, http://www.towleroad.com/2014/09/brooklynattack.html.

Renninger, B. J. 2015. "'Where I Can Be Myself … Where I Can Speak My Mind': Networked Counterpublics in a Polymedia Environment." *New Media and Society* 17 (9): 1513–1529.

Rivett, M. 1999. "Misfit Lit: 'Punk Writing' and Representations of Punk through Writing and Publishing." In *Punk Rock So What? The Cultural Legacy of Punk*, ed. R. Sabin, 31–48. London: Routledge.

Rothbauer, P. 2005. "Practice of Everyday Life." In *Theories of Information Behavior*, ed. K. E. Fisher, S. Erdelez, and L. McKechnie, 284–288. Medford, NJ: American Society for Information Science and Technology by Information Today.

Rupp, R. 2014. "The Search for Immortality in Food." *National Geographic*, October 30, http://theplate.nationalgeographic.com/2014/10/30/immortality-food-diet-for-a-long-life.

Rybas, N., and R. Gajjala. 2007. "Developing Cyberethnographic Research Methods for Understanding Digitally Mediated Identities." *Forum: Qualitative Social Research / Sozialforschung* 8 (3): 1–15.

Satchell, C., and P. Dourish. 2009. "Beyond the User: Use and Non-use in HCI." In *OZCHI '09: Proceedings of the Twenty-first Annual Conference of the Australian Computer-Human Interaction Special Interest Group: Design: Open 24/7*, ed. M. Foth, 9–16. New York: ACM.

Schroeder, R. 2014. "Big Data and the Brave New World of Social Media Research." *Big Data and Society* 1 (2), http://bds.sagepub.com/content/1/2/2053951714563194.

Seals, G. 2014. "Facebook Tells Drag Queens to Use Their Legal Names or Risk Losing Their Profiles." *The Daily Dot,* September 11, http://www.dailydot.com/lifestyle/facebook-demands-drag-queens-change-names.

Sennett, R. 2008. *The Craftsman.* New Haven, CT: Yale University Press.

Silverstone, R. 2006. *Media and Morality: On the Rise of the Mediapolis.* Cambridge, UK: Polity Press.

Sinnreich, A. 2010. *Mashed Up: Music, Technology, and the Rise of Configurable Culture.* Amherst: University of Massachusetts Press.

Slaughter, D. 2016. "New Bill Would Create a Registry of All the Bands and DJs That Play Philly: 'It's Become Necessary.'" *BillyPenn,* January 27, http://billypenn.com/2016/01/27/new-bill-would-create-a-registry-of-all-the-bands-and-djs-that-play-philly-its-become-necessary.

Solove, D. J. 2011. *Nothing to Hide: The False Tradeoff between Privacy and Security.* New Haven, CT: Yale University Press.

Star, S. L. 1990. "Power, Technology and the Phenomenology of Conventions: On Being Allergic to Onions." *Sociological Review* 38: 26–56.

Stefik, M. 1997. *Internet Dreams: Archetypes, Myths, and Metaphors.* Cambridge, MA: MIT Press.

Talja, S., K. Tuominen, and R. Savolainen. 2005. "'Isms' in Information Science: Constructivism, Collectivism and Constructionism." *Journal of Documentation* 61 (1): 79–101.

Taussig, M. T. 2012. *Beauty and the Beast.* Chicago: University of Chicago Press.

Thornton, S. 2013. *Club Cultures: Music, Media and Subcultural Capital.* New York: Wiley.

Tracer, D. 2014. "Facebook Targeting Drag Queens, Forcing Them to Use Their Legal Names." Queerty, September 11, http://www.queerty.com/facebook-targeting-drag-queens-forcing-them-to-use-their-legal-names-20140911.

Travers, M. 2001. *Qualitative Research through Case Studies.* London: Sage.

Turner, F. 2006. *From Counterculture to Cyberculture.* Chicago: University of Chicago Press.

Turow, J. 2011. *The Daily You: How the New Advertising Industry Is Defining Your Identity and Your Worth.* New Haven, CT: Yale University Press.

U.S. Census Bureau. 2010. "Quick Facts: New York City, NY." http://www.census.gov/quickfacts/table/PST045215/3651000.

U.S. Department of Health and Human Services. n.d. "Mandated Reporting." https://www.childwelfare.gov/responding/reporting/mandated.

U.S. Department of Justice. n.d. "Citizen's Guide to U.S. Federal Law in Obscenity." https://www.justice.gov/criminal-ceos/citizens-guide-us-federal-law-obscenity.

Vaidhyanathan, S. 2008. "Generational Myth." *Chronicle of Higher Education*, September 19, http://chronicle.com/article/Generational-Myth/32491.

Veinot, T. C., and K. Williams. 2012. "Following the 'Community' Thread from Sociology to Information Behavior and Informatics: Uncovering Theoretical Continuities and Research Opportunities." *Journal of the American Society for Information Science and Technology* 63 (5): 847–864.

Wajcman, J. 2004. *Technofeminism*. Cambridge, UK: Polity.

Waksman, S. 2004. "California Noise: Tinkering with Hardcore and Heavy Metal in Southern California." *Social Studies of Science* 34 (5): 675–702.

Wellman, B. 1997. "The Road to Utopia and Dystopia on the Information Highway." *Contemporary Sociology* 26 (4): 445–449. Retrieved from http://www.jstor.org/stable/2655085.

Wenger, E. 1998. *Communities of Practice: Learning, Meaning, and Identity*. Cambridge, UK: Cambridge University Press.

Weston, K. 1991. *Families We Choose: Lesbians, Gays, Kinship*. New York: Columbia University Press.

Williams, R. 1991. "Base and Superstructure in Marxist Cultural Theory." In *Rethinking Popular Culture: Contemporary Perspectives in Cultural Studies*, ed. C. Mukerji and M. Schudson, 465–486. Berkeley: University of California Press.

Winner, L. 1986. *The Whale and the Reactor: A Search for Limits in an Age of High Technology*. Chicago, IL: University of Chicago Press.

Wolfson, T. 2014. *Digital Rebellion: The Birth of the Cyber Left*. Chicago: University of Illinois Press.

Wongsurawat, W. 2005. "Pornography and Social Ills: Evidence from the Early 1990s." *Journal of Applied Econometrics* 9 (1): 185–213.

Yaniv, O., and R. Paranscandola. 2014. "Five Men Arrested for Gang Assault against Black Gay Brooklyn Man." *Daily News*, April 23, http://www.nydailynews.com/new-york/nyc-crime/men-arrested-israel-bias-attack-gay-black-man-article-1.1766106.

Index

Note: Page numbers in *italic* type refer to illustrations.